THREE PLAYS

THREE PLAYS

The Political Theater of Howard Zinn

EMMA
MARX IN SOHO
DAUGHTER OF VENUS

———

Howard Zinn

BEACON PRESS, BOSTON

BEACON PRESS
25 Beacon Street
Boston, Massachusetts 02108-2892
www.beacon.org

Beacon Press books
are published under the auspices of
the Unitarian Universalist Association of Congregations.

To obtain permission for creative performances of *Emma* or *Marx in Soho,* please write
to Howard Zinn, c/o South End Press, 7 Brookline Street,
Suite 1, Cambridge, MA 02139; for *Daughter of Venus,* please write to
Howard Zinn, c/o Beacon Press, 25 Beacon Street, Boston, MA 02108.

This book is printed on acid-free paper that meets the uncoated paper
ANSI/NISO specifications for permanence as revised in 1992.

Text design and composition by Tag Savage
at Wilsted & Taylor Publishing Services.

Library of Congress Cataloging-in-Publication Data

Zinn, Howard,
[Plays. Selections]
Three plays : the political theater of Howard Zinn :
Emma, Marx in Soho, Daughter of Venus / Howard Zinn.
p. cm.
Includes bibliographical references.
ISBN 978-0-8070-7326-1 (pbk. : alk. paper)
1. Political plays, American. 2. Goldman, Emma, 1869–1940—
Drama. 3. Marx, Karl, 1818–1883—Drama. I. Title.
PS3576.I538A6 2010
812'.54—dc22   2009035943

CONTENTS

Introduction
vii

EMMA

Preface   3
Emma   17

MARX IN SOHO:
A PLAY ON HISTORY

Preface   103
Marx in Soho: A Play on History   113

DAUGHTER OF VENUS

Preface   145
Daughter of Venus   149

INTRODUCTION

Why would a historian move outside the boundaries of the discipline (refuse to be disciplined) and decide to enter the world of the theater—that is, to write plays? I can't speak for others—the historian Martin Duberman is the only one who comes to mind, having written the documentary play *In White America* during the early years of the civil rights movement.

In my case, it was something I had in mind for a long time, because even as I was writing history, my family was involved in the theater. In 1961, when I was teaching at Spelman College in Atlanta, my wife, Roslyn, was cast as Anna, the English schoolteacher, in a black production of *The King and I*. She went on to play a number of roles for Theater Atlanta, including the role of Miss Madrigal in Enid Bagnold's *The Chalk Garden*. When we moved to Boston, she was cast in Bertolt Brecht's *The Caucasian Chalk Circle* at Harvard's Loeb Theater (predecessor of the American Repertory Theater). In Atlanta, my daughter Myla was chosen, over sixty contenders, for the role of Anne Frank and was cited as Best Actress of the Year in 1962. My son Jeff worked as an actor and director in New York, then moved to Cape Cod and became artistic director of the Wellfleet Harbor Actors Theater (W.H.A.T.).

So I was left behind, to wander in libraries and engage in the solitary pursuit of writing history, while observing the rest of my family having fun in the theater. Always the longing was there, perhaps having begun as far back as when I was sixteen and saw my first play in a funky little theater in Manhattan.

It was a Federal Theater Project production of *One Third of a Nation,* getting its title from FDR's famous declaration "I see one-third of a nation ill-housed, ill-clad, ill-nourished." My family fit that description, living in various dingy tenements in Brooklyn. As I sat on a wooden bench (could I expect more, having paid 17 cents for admission?) waiting for the play to begin in the darkened theater, I heard the sirens of fire engines, growing louder and louder, and then saw flames shooting up frighteningly from the stage, where one could make out a tenement building on fire. I soon realized it was all a fake but a marvelously exciting way to introduce the theme of the play—poor people made homeless by fire sweeping through wooden tenements.

That experience suggested to me, early on, the power of drama in conveying a message of social significance. It began a life-long fascination with the stage. When we lived in a low-income housing project in downtown Manhattan, my wife and I would scrape together some money to see Broadway plays. We could only afford the cheapest seats. Still, we were thrilled to see the original productions of *A Streetcar Named Desire, Native Son, Death of a Salesman, All My Sons.*

When we moved south, to live in the black community of the Atlanta colleges, and I became involved in the movement against racial segregation, I experienced the theater vicariously through my family. Moving north, my life centered around teaching history and politics at Boston University, but even more, around the struggle to end the war in Vietnam. Writing about war and civil disobedience, I had no chance to think about writing for the theater. But when the war in Vietnam ended, and I was no longer racing around the country for lectures and demonstrations against the war, I felt free to write my first play, *Emma,* about the outrageous feminist-anarchist Emma Goldman, her comrades, her lovers. I now experienced an excitement that could never be matched in the world of the university. I discovered that writing for the theater had a quality missing in the writing of books and articles. Those were solitary endeavors, but when you wrote a play it quickly became a collective experience.

As soon as you, the playwright, turned over your script to a director, it was no longer a lone creative act. Almost immediately, the play belonged to the director, the actors, the set designer, the lighting and costume people, the stage manager, as much as it did to you. And there was a passion binding all of you together in a collective effort to bring your words to the stage in the most dramatic, most compelling way possible. It was an emotional experience unlike anything I had ever known as a professor, as an author of historical works. I was going to be working with all these other people, intensely, in close quarters, with a warmth and affection foreign to academe. People arrived for rehearsal and hugged one another. It was not a scene one encountered in the university.

But would writing for the theater be as satisfying, for someone like me, whose life and writing had been concentrated on war, law, poverty, injustice, racism? Thinking about it, I concluded that neither form of social struggle could be considered superior. Each had its unique power. Writing historical and political works, I could introduce to my readers ideas and facts that might provoke them to examine anew the world around them, and decide to join the fray. Writing plays would zoom in on a few characters, and by getting the viewers to identify with them emotionally, move the audience in a visceral way, something not easily achievable in prosaic works of history and political philosophy.

A play, like any other form of artistic expression (novels, poetry, music, painting), has the possibility of transcendence. It can, by an imaginative reconstruction of reality, transcend the conventional wisdom, transcend orthodoxy, transcend the word of the establishment, escape what is handed down by our culture, challenge the boundaries of race, class, religion, nation. Art dares to start from scratch, from the core of human need, from feelings that are not represented in what we call reality. The French reb-els of 1968 posted a slogan: *"Soyez realiste. Demandez l'impossible"* ("Be realistic. Demand the impossible."). Centuries earlier Pascal said: "The heart has its reasons, which reason cannot know."

That is the goal, which not all art attains. And certainly, my writing of plays would fall short of the potential for an imagi-native reconstruction of reality. But I would have something to strive for, something outside the disciplines of history and politi-cal philosophy. And, I concluded, especially after my first experi-ence in theater, this would be more fun than the lone pursuit of history.

Emma was first performed in New York in 1977 at the The-ater for the New City, and was directed by my son, Jeff Zinn. The following year, in Boston, it was directed by the Obie Award win-ner Maxine Klein, with an ensemble of talented performers who had been a successful improvisational group before they turned to the theater. *Emma* ran for eight months, the longest-running play in Boston in 1977. In the eighties it played in New York again, directed by Maxine Klein; then in London, at the Young Vic; and at the Edinburgh Festival, directed by Pauline Randall. In 1990, translated into Japanese, it was performed in Tokyo and other Japanese cities. More recently, in various translations, it has played in Germany, France, Spain, and Argentina.

In the early 1980s, I wrote my second play, *Daughter of Ve-nus,* which was first performed in New York in 1984, directed by Jeff Zinn at the Theater for the New City, whose artistic di-rectors, Crystal Field and George Bartenieff, were doing some of the most creative theater work in the city. Jeff Zinn directed it again the following year at the White Barn Theater in Nor-walk, Connecticut. In 2008, the revised script had a reading at Kate Snodgrass's Boston Playwrights Theater, directed by David Wheeler, and the following year it had a full performance there and at Suffolk University in Boston, directed by Wesley Savick.

As for *Marx in Soho,* after a reading in Boston at the Boston Playwrights Theater, it was performed in 1995 in Providence, Rhode Island, and then in Washington, D.C. Since then it has been staged in several hundred venues in the United States, performed variously by Brian Jones, Jerry Levy, and Bob Weick. In 2009 it was performed at the Central Square Theater in Cambridge, Massachusetts, directed by David Wheeler. Translated into Spanish, French, Italian, and German, it has played in a number of European cities, as well as in Havana and other venues in Latin America. After being translated into Greek it was done in various cities by the distinguished Greek actor Aggelos Antonopoulos and directed by Athanasia Karagiannopoulou. I was invited to Athens in 2009 to see the performance, before an audience of a thousand, at the University of Athens.

Emma and *Marx in Soho* were published by South End Press, with the aid of one of its editorial collective, Anthony Arnove. *Daughter of Venus* remained unpublished until now, and I am grateful to Helene Atwan and Beacon Press for agreeing to publish all three of my plays in this one volume.

EMMA

PREFACE

I was introduced to Emma Goldman (though not personally) by a fellow historian, Richard Drinnon, whom I met at a conference in Pennsylvania in the early 1960s. He told me he had written a biography of her called *Rebel in Paradise*. When I returned home, I found the book and read it, more and more fascinated by this astonishing figure in American history. It struck me that in all of my work in American history, whether in undergraduate or graduate school, her name had never come up.

This was an experience I was to have many times after I left school and began to read about people and events that somehow never fit into the traditional history curriculum: Mother Jones, Big Bill Haywood, John Reed, the Ludlow Massacre, the Lawrence Textile Strike, the Haymarket Affair, and much more. The people it was considered important to study were presidents, industrialists, military heroes—not labor leaders, radicals, socialists, anarchists. Emma Goldman did not fit.

I was led to read Emma's autobiography, *Living My Life*. Then I turned to the works of the Russian anarchists Peter Kropotkin and Mikhail Bakunin. I became interested in anarchism as a political philosophy, and discovered that it was outside the pale of orthodox political theory as taught in the academic world.

Coming to the faculty of Boston University in the fall of 1964, I was introduced to another new faculty member whose field was philosophy. Learning that I was joining the political science department, he asked: "And what is your political philosophy?"

I replied, half seriously, "Anarchism."

He looked at me sharply and said: "Impossible!"

In 1974, while I was teaching in Paris, I made a trip to Amsterdam and visited the International Institute of Social History. There I found a treasure trove of letters between Emma Goldman and Alexander Berkman, written in Europe after they were deported from the United States at the close of the First World War. I copied as much as I could on rough pieces of note paper, but when I returned home I found that Richard and Anna Maria Drinnon had gone through the same material and had just published a selection of the Goldman—Berkman correspondence, by the title *Nowhere at Home*.

Through the 1960s and early 1970s, much of my life had been taken up with the movement against the war in Vietnam—speaking, participating in demonstrations, traveling to Japan and to Vietnam, writing about the American invasion of Southeast Asia. When the war ended in 1975, I finally found time to do what I had been wanting to do for a long time, to write a play about the magnificent Emma Goldman. My son, Jeff, an actor given his first directing assignment by the Theater for the New City in Manhattan, offered to direct the first production of the play in 1976.

The following year, rewritten (as it has been after every production), it played in Boston, directed by Maxine Klein, with the ensemble group "The Next Move" forming the cast. It received glowing reviews, played for eight months, and was seen by about twenty thousand people. In the years that followed, it played again in New York, then in London and in Tokyo. One version of it was published by the South End Press as part of a collection of feminist plays called *Playbook*. The play, of necessity, can only cover a part of Emma Goldman's remarkable life story. She

was born in Kovno, Lithuania, which was then part of Russia, in
1869, and in her memoir recalls both the miseries of life in a poor
Jewish family and the rare moments of excitement that punctu-
ated that life. Always open to passionate encounters, she tells of
her first erotic experience, as a little girl being thrown into the air
and caught again and again by a young man of the village. She
tells also of being taken to the opera while visiting a prosperous
aunt in Konigsberg and weeping as one of Verdi's beautiful arias
filled the concert hall.

Her family emigrated to the United States and lived in Rochester, New York, amidst the Jewish immigrant culture. At sixteen,
Emma was working in a factory. She was abruptly married off to a
young man she did not love and who was unable to consummate
the marriage. Her father was a tyrant. So she learned early of the
subordination of women, to husbands, to fathers. But she was a
reader, and a dreamer. At seventeen, she became aware of the labor struggles in Chicago for an eight-hour day. In these struggles,
the Haymarket Affair of 1886 played a central role.

Its origin was in a strike against the International Harvester
Company, during which police killed several strikers. The anarchist movement in Chicago, which was formidable, called for a
protest meeting in Haymarket Square. The meeting was peaceful,
but when a small army of police decided to break it up, a bomb
exploded in the police ranks, wounding sixty-six policemen, of
whom seven later died. The police then fired into the crowd, killing several people and wounding two hundred.

There was no evidence on who threw the bomb (and to this
day it remains a mystery), but the police arrested eight anarchist
leaders in Chicago. A jury found them guilty on the supposi-
tion that whoever threw the bomb must have been influenced by
the incendiary statements of the anarchists, whose circulars, after
the International Harvester shootings, called for "Revenge!" The
eight were sentenced to death by hanging.

This became an event of international excitement. Meetings took place all over Europe in defense of the condemned men. When their appeal was turned down by the Illinois Supreme Court, George Bernard Shaw responded: "If the world must lose eight of its people, it can better afford to lose the eight members of the Illinois Supreme Court." One of the men blew himself up in his cell. Three were later pardoned by Governor John Peter Altgeld (who later became the subject of a historical novel by Howard Fast called *The American*). Four were hanged.

These events had a tumultuous emotional effect on the young Emma. She decided to leave her family in Rochester, leave her job and her husband behind, and go to New York, where she could find the freedom to live her own life. There she met a group of young anarchists, among them Alexander Berkman, also an immigrant from Russia and ferociously devoted to the cause of creating a new society. Emma and Sasha (as Berkman was known to his friends) became lovers.

A powerful influence on both Emma and Sasha was the famous German revolutionary, Johann Most, who had been in the Reichstag, had spent time in prison, and now used his eloquence on the public platform to advance the cause of anarchism. Most was taken with the young, passionate comrade, and this led to some tension between Emma and Sasha.

Emma found work in a factory and began organizing the immigrant workers (most of them women) in Manhattan. In 1892, workers in Homestead, Pennsylvania, initiated a strike against one of Andrew Carnegie's steel mills, managed by the ruthless Henry Clay Frick (later to become, like Carnegie, a philanthropist). Frick hired the Pinkerton Detective Agency, the largest strikebreaking agency in the nation, and at one point its operatives opened fire with rifles and machine guns, killing seven strikers.

Aroused by this, Emma, Sasha, and several of their comrades decided on a bold act of vengeance, to show the world that the titans of industry were not invulnerable. They would assassinate Henry Clay Frick.

Sasha, willing to sacrifice himself for the good of the cause, insisted on carrying out the act alone. He traveled to Pittsburgh, burst into Frick's office, and fired away. Sasha was hardly an experienced assassin. His shots only managed to wound Frick, and he was overpowered. The trial was quick, and Sasha was sentenced to twenty-two years in the Pennsylvania State Penitentiary. His account of that experience, *Prison Memoirs of an Anarchist*, is a classic of prison writing.

Life in prison was an endless torment, especially since Sasha continued to defy the authorities in many ways and was repeatedly punished. Other prisoners had committed suicide rather than endure the cruelties of imprisonment, and Sasha was not sure he would last out his time. His desperation was conveyed to Emma and his friends, and they concocted a bizarre plan for his escape. They rented a house not far from the prison walls and began to dig a tunnel that would come up in the prison yard, with a comrade playing a piano to drown out the sounds of digging.

But just at the time they finished their work, the tunnel was discovered and Sasha was severely punished. While Berkman was in prison, Emma continued to organize and agitate. In 1893, a terrible year of economic crisis, when children in the cities were dying of hunger and sickness, she addressed a huge demonstration in Union Square and urged her listeners to invade the food stores and take what they needed to feed their families—rather than waiting for legislation or petitioning the authorities. This was a vivid illustration of the anarchist principle of "direct action." Emma was dragged off the speakers' platform by the police and was sentenced to two years on Blackwell's Island.

In prison, Emma learned nursing and midwifery. This training was to be useful for the rest of her life. (In E.L. Doctorow's novel *Ragtime* there is a brilliantly written scene of Emma giving a massage to a showgirl of that era.)

While Sasha was enduring prison, Emma was rapidly becoming known as a leading orator and organizer in the labor and anarchist movements.

When President William McKinley was shot and killed in 1901 by a man named Leon Czolgosz, Emma had to hide out because the police immediately, and mistakenly, assumed she was involved in the assassination.

In fact, Emma Goldman no longer believed, as she did at the time of the Frick event, that assassination was justified in the cause of anarchism, but she refused to heap abuse on Czolgosz, as some of her radical friends did, arguing that, however irrational his act, people had to understand that there were legitimate reasons for his anger.

Through all this time, in keeping with her philosophy of freedom in love, Emma had various lovers, even while she retained enormous affection and admiration for Alexander Berkman. When he finally came out of prison in 1906, their friendship was renewed, but they were no longer sexually intimate. They remained comrades in the cause of anarchism and together founded the journal *Mother Earth*.

In 1908, while lecturing in Chicago, Emma encountered for the first time the amazing Ben Reitman, in what would become the most tumultuous emotional experience of her life. He was Dr. Ben Reitman, having made his way somehow through medical school, but he was as far from the traditional physician as one could imagine. He was dark-haired and handsome, a man who dressed flamboyantly and opened a storefront clinic in Chicago where hobos, prostitutes, and poor people in general could come for help. He performed abortions and otherwise flouted the rules of the profession and of society.

Reitman was a man of ferocious sexual appetites, and he and Emma fell passionately in love. Their correspondence, only discovered in recent years, is among the most torrid and explicit in the annals of letter-writing. She was thirty-nine and he was twenty-nine, but the difference in age was clearly not important to them. In *Living My Life*, Emma describes meeting Reitman:

> He arrived in the afternoon, an exotic, picturesque figure with a large black cowboy hat, flowing silk tie, and huge cane. . . . His voice was deep, soft, and ingratiating. . . . [He was] a tall man with a finely shaped head, covered with a mass of curly black hair, which evidently had not been washed for some time. His eyes were brown, large, and dreamy. His lips, disclosing beautiful teeth when he smiled, were full and passionate. He looked a handsome brute. . . . I could not take my eyes off his hands.[1]

Shortly after meeting Reitman, Emma wrote to him: "You have opened up the prison gates of my womanhood. . . . [I]f I were asked to choose between a world of understanding and the spring that fills my body with fire, I should have to choose the spring."[2]

Emma was soon in thrall to her overwhelming physical need for Reitman. He was traveling with Emma, managing her lectures, but also ready for adventures with other women. Yet she could not break the tie. She wrote to him at one point:

> If ever our correspondence should be published, the world would stand aghast that I, Emma Goldman, the strong revolu-

---

1. Boston University Library Special Collections, *Emma Goldman Papers*, Collection #243, Boxes 1, 2, 3. See also *The Emma Goldman Papers: A Microfilm Edition* (Ann Arbor, MI: Chadwyck-Healey, 1991), Reels 6, 7, and 68; *Emma Goldman: A Guide to Her Life and Documentary Sources* (Ann Arbor, MI: Chadwyck-Healey, 1995); *Emma Goldman: The American Years* (Berkeley: University of California Press, 2003); and documents available at the Emma Goldman Papers Project, University of California, Berkeley; http://sunsite.berkeley.edu/Goldman/.
2. Candace Falk, *Love, Anarchy, and Emma Goldman* (New York: Holt, Rinehart, and Winston, 1984), 4.

tionist, the daredevil, the one who has defied laws and conven-
tion, should have been as helpless as a shipwrecked crew on a
foaming ocean.[3]

Yet Emma Goldman did not stop her endless speaking, agitating, organizing. She seemed to be tireless as she traveled the
country, lecturing to large audiences everywhere, on birth control ("A woman should decide for herself."), on the problems of
marriage as an institution ("Marriage has nothing to do with
love."), on patriotism ("the last refuge of a scoundrel"), on free
love ("What is love if not free?"), and also on the drama—Shaw,
Ibsen, Strindberg.

She was arrested again and again, simply for speaking. In
Chicago in 1908 police dragged her off the stage. A reporter for
the *Chicago Daily Tribune* recorded this dialogue:

> "Thought you'd come here and make trouble, eh?" the Captain
> [said] . . .
>
> "Behave yourself," said Miss Goldman sharply. "Talk like a man,
> even if you are a policeman."[4]

In one month in 1909, police broke up eleven of her meetings.
In San Francisco, she spoke to five thousand people on patriotism, with the crowd blocking off the police until they retreated.[5]
In San Diego, a mob kidnapped Ben Reitman, took him out of
town, tarred and feathered him, and branded his buttocks with
the initials "I.W.W." But (a tribute to his courage, as well as to
hers) the two of them returned later to San Diego for Emma
to give her talk.

---

3. Ibid.
4. Ibid., 65.
5. Goldman, *Living My Life*, Vol. 1, 427–28. The talk, "Patriotism: A Men-
   ace to Liberty," appears in Goldman, *Anarchism and Other Essays*, 127–44.

Emma's sexual freedom may well have gone so far as to permit a brief erotic relationship with a woman in New Kensington, Pennsylvania. The woman was Almeda Sperry. Though she is not mentioned in Emma's autobiography, I came across a batch of letters from Almeda to Emma in the special collections of the Boston University Library. Almeda was an extraordinary person, a working-class woman who gave of her body to men when she needed money, who loved theater and opera, and who set up a socialist group in New Kensington.

Almeda Sperry's letters to Emma are remarkable for their passionate declarations of affections, their intense social consciousness, their insights into the life of a woman struggling to survive, and her exultant love for opera, theater, and literature. When I read them, I knew I must somehow recreate her presence in my play, even if only through one of her letters, as she describes an encounter with Ben Reitman. Here is a passage from another letter:

> I wonder if everyone is as dippy as I am about shows. . . . I almost committed suicide when Sara Bernhardt was to come here last and I was broke, but Fred gave me a dollar and I got a seat in goose heaven. What a voice Sara has—what a golden, liquid voice and what enunciation. I have practiced her rage in La Tosca in front of the looking glass. . . . Wouldn't it be grand, Emma, if the government would run the theatres and let the people in for nothing. . . . If I could go to a good show every night I'd work for just my grub and enuf clothes to hide my nakedness and I'd be kind to everybody.[6]

Reitman and Emma had ten tempestuous years together, during which Emma, despite her emotional turmoil, managed to maintain an extraordinary level of political activity, culminating

---

6. See note 1.

in her opposition to American entrance into the war in 1917. That event also marked their breakup. Reitman, though he had shown personal courage in many ways, had no desire to risk his freedom by overt opposition to the war.

Emma and Alexander Berkman, comrades throughout it all, defied the law by denouncing conscription and the war, and were sentenced to prison in 1918. When the war was over, they were released, only to be deported, along with many other radicals, in the fierce repression that accompanied the war's end. At the start of his infamous career as a right-wing fanatic, J. Edgar Hoover himself supervised their deportation, on a boat bound for Russia, their birthplace.

It was no longer Tsarist Russia, however, but the new Soviet Union, in which Lenin had dissolved the Constituent Assembly, representing many political factions, and instituted the rule of the Bolsheviks. Emma and Sasha, meeting with Lenin and Trotsky, observing the jailing of dissidents, the breakup of demonstrations, and, finally, the bloody crushing of the sailors' revolt in Kronstadt, outside of Petrograd, could not bear the idea of remaining in the Soviet Union.

They spent their remaining years in various parts of Europe, especially on the Mediterranean coast of France, writing to one another endlessly (many of these letters are preserved in the collection by Richard and Anna Maria Drinnon), keeping in touch with events in Europe and the United States, lending their names and their support to whatever good causes moved them. Emma traveled to Spain during the civil war there and spoke in 1936 to enormous crowds in Barcelona, which was briefly an anarchist enclave (described vividly in George Orwell's *Homage to Catalonia*).

Berkman, seriously ill and in pain, took his own life in 1936. Emma made a rare trip to the United States in 1940, through the offices of Frances Perkins, Roosevelt's progressive secretary of labor. The condition was that she only speak about the drama, and so she gave a series of lectures on Ibsen, Shaw, Strindberg, and Chekhov. But, on a brief stop in Canada, she became ill and died. She was seventy-one.

The 1960s marked a revival of interest in anarchism. One reason was a fierce hostility to the American government. The federal government had collaborated for almost one hundred years in maintaining racial segregation in the South. That collaboration only came to an end (at least legally) when black people took to the streets in Georgia, Alabama, Mississippi, and the other Southern states and embarrassed the nation before the entire world.

The same government was waging a brutal war in Southeast Asia, the longest war in the country's history. It only began to retreat from that in the face of fierce resistance in Vietnam and a huge national antiwar movement in the United States.

The radicals of the 1960s were not, like those of the 1930s, connected to the Communist movement or admirers of the Soviet Union. They called themselves "the New Left," and there was a strong ideological and emotional connection to anarchism, even though the term itself was not much used. The connection was not just a suspicion of all governments, but a belief in what the Students for a Democratic Society and others called "participatory democracy."

The movements of the 1960s seemed to embody the anarchist principle of decentralized organization, as opposed to the party discipline of the Old Left. The Student Nonviolent Coordinating Committee was made up of small groups, young and mostly black, working in the most dangerous parts of the Deep South, embedding themselves in local communities, and maintaining only occasional contact with the national office in Atlanta.

The feminist movement of those years, also without talking about anarchism, acted on the anarchist principle of decentralized organization, working day by day in small women's groups throughout the country. From time to time, there would be parades and national demonstrations on behalf of sexual equality, but women were not bound to any one charismatic leader.

What also connected the movements of the 1960s to the historic philosophy of anarchism was the idea of direct action. This meant that social change would not be sought by political parties striving to take over government, but by citizens banding together and acting directly against the source of their oppression.

Historically, the labor movement, when it was not held back by conservative national leadership, had engaged in such action: strikes, directly against the employer, had won the eight-hour day. The government could not be counted on to do anything for working people. It was controlled by the rich and powerful, tied to corporate power. So workers had to do the job themselves.

The Southern civil rights movement used the slogan "nonviolent direct action" to describe its campaign of sit-ins and freedom rides. When antiwar activists blocked streets in Washington, D.C., surrounded the Pentagon, and broke into draft boards, they were engaging in direct action. The various acts of civil disobedience by dissidents, in challenging the law and the government, were consonant with anarchist philosophy, whether the participants knew this or not.

Anarchism as a philosophy, which had great influence in the late nineteenth and early twentieth centuries, in Europe and also in the United States, was overshadowed after 1917 by the Communist movement and its attachment to the Soviet Union. With the movements of the 1960s, this changed. The new antistate politics, as well as the culture of freedom, in music, in sex, in communal living, led to a revival of interest in anarchism. Emma Goldman, after decades of obscurity, now became an admired figure, especially in the women's movement, but also in the other political and other movements of that time.

It was in the late 1960s that I began using anarchist writings in my course in political theory at Boston University. My students were reading Emma's autobiography, *Living My Life,* as well as a collection of her lectures, *Anarchism and Other Essays.* Sometimes I used a short book by Alexander Berkman, which was a concise and simple explanation of anarchist ideas, called *The ABC of Anarchism.* I began teaching a seminar, "Marxism and Anarchism."

When *Emma* was first produced in New York and Boston, it covered the events of Emma Goldman's life up to the year 1906, when Alexander Berkman came out of prison. I knew about Emma's relationship with Ben Reitman, but when Candace Falk published her book *Love, Anarchy, and Emma Goldman,* reproducing the astonishing love letters between Emma and Ben, I felt I had to bring this swashbuckling character into my play. And so, when the play was performed in London in 1987, Reitman became one of the characters, and the story was carried into the First World War.

For the English production, we changed the title of the play, because Jane Austen's novel *Emma* was so well known to English audiences. We now called the play *Rebel in Paradise,* with Richard Drinnon kindly consenting to our use of the title of his biography of Emma. When the play opened in Tokyo in 1990, however, we returned to the original title.

EMMA

Act One | Scene One

Overture: "Mein Ruhe Platz," on the piano, or, if taped, sung in chorus. A factory whistle is heard in the dark. As the lights come up, four women, of various ages—Emma, Rose, Jenny, Dora—are sitting at their imaginary machines, going through the motions of sewing, their feet working the treadle, making a steady beat, one hand working the material through, the other hand turning the wheel, and, every few turns, without losing the rhythm, quickly wiping the sweat from their foreheads. They work silently, quickly, with excruciating regularity, and the only sound we hear is the rhythmic sound of feet on the floor, simulating the treadle. Then one of the women begins to sing "Mein Ruhe Platz." She sings two stanzas, and then the foreman, Vogel, appears (or his voice is heard offstage), an excitable man, not unkind but fearful and nervous about his responsibility.

VOGEL: How many times do I have to tell you? No singing on the job. Please!
 (The woman stops singing.)
VOGEL: Who wants to sing, get a job with the opera! *(He shakes his head, leaves.)*
 (The women continue working in silence. When they do speak, they do it without breaking the work rhythm.)
JENNY: You remember the fire at Kachinsky's shop last month?

DORA: Eighteen girls died. Some burned to death. Some jumped from windows. Who can forget such a thing?

JENNY: Well, it said in the paper this morning why those girls couldn't get down the back stairs.

DORA: So?

JENNY: The door was locked from the outside. Kachinsky locked it because a few girls were sneaking out on the roof for a little air.

DORA: The dirty bastard! And he calls himself a Jew.

ROSE: Is a Jewish boss any different?

DORA: A Jew is supposed to be different.

ROSE: They're all the same, believe me. I've worked for Jews, Gentiles—even Italians.

JENNY: I don't feel good working here on the eighth floor. There's too many fires these days. Did you read what the fire chief of New York said?

DORA: Who reads all that foolishness?

JENNY: You better read. He says his ladders only reach up to the sixth floor. If you're on the seventh or eighth, like us, pray to God.

(They all stop working the machines, there is no motion, no sound for a few seconds, then slowly they start up again.)

ROSE: You know, the back door on this floor is locked from the outside too—

JENNY: What are you saying?

ROSE: It's been that way ever since I've been working here.

DORA: That's not right.

ROSE: It's better not to think about it.

JENNY: Someone should tell Vogel to open the door.

DORA: You talk, you get in trouble. Who'll tell Vogel? Not me.

(They keep working in silence.)

EMMA *(loudly, startling the others)*: Mr. Vogel! Please! Go outside and open the back door. In case of a fire . . .

VOGEL *(off) (a man who gets excited quickly)*: Mind your own business! *(Vogel appears.)* You work on the corsets. It's Mr. Handlin's shop. I have nothing to do with doors. Emma, take my advice. You're the youngest girl here. Learn to mind your own business.

EMMA *(getting up from the machine)*: I'm not working if the door is locked.

VOGEL *(even more excited now)*: Good! Good! Leave! Go home right now. Who needs you? *(He is a great gesticulator.)* Dora, you stay a little later tonight and do Emma's work. You'll get paid extra. We have to finish this order tonight. Mr. Handlin is waiting for it.

DORA *(softly)*: I can't stay later.

VOGEL *(pointing)*: You, Jenny.

JENNY: I have to be home on time tonight.

VOGEL *(desperately)*: Rose!

 (Rose shakes her head.)

VOGEL *(shouting)*: What's the matter with all of you?

ROSE: The door. You have to open the door.

VOGEL: I'm not supposed to. It's not my business.

 (Emma starts to leave.)

DORA: Emma, wait for me. *(Gets up from the machine)* Mr. Vogel, I'm sorry, I'm scared of fires.

JENNY: Me too. *(Gets up)*

ROSE: Mr. Vogel, if there's a fire, you won't be able to get down the stairs either.

VOGEL: You're all meshugah.

 (They've all stopped working.)

VOGEL: What are you doing to me? Please, girls, I've got a family to support. Please, back to the machines, the order has to get out tonight.

EMMA: Open the door!

ALL: Open the door!

VOGEL *(shouting)*: All right! Enough! All right! *(He goes off. We hear the sound of the latch opening and Vogel still shouting.)* You're satisfied? I'll lose my job and then you'll be satisfied! All right, back to work!

> *(The women go back to the rhythm of the machines, working silently, only the sound of their shoes on the foot pedals. Then, after the silence . . .)*

DORA: A friend of mine saw the fire at Kachinsky's shop. . . . The girls on the tenth floor came out on the window ledge, the flames all around them. They looked so small up there. And when their clothes began to burn, they jumped. Two of them, three of them, at a time—holding hands . . .

> *(Silence, as they work the machines. Then one of them starts humming "Mein Ruhe Platz" and the others join in, one by one, all humming and working the machines.)*

Scene Two

In the darkness, a happy Yiddish tune plays. Lights up on the Goldman kitchen. Emma and her sister Helena are dancing. Helena teaching Emma, both laughing. Mother preparing food. Father nodding his head to the music. Mr. Levine enters, a well-off distant relative in the dress business.

FATHER: Hello, Mr. Levine! Emma . . .

> *(She turns.)*

FATHER: Stop dancing and say hello to Mr. Levine. Helena, you too!

> *(Emma and Helena's faces show their distaste for Levine as they look at one another as if to say: "There he is again.")*

LEVINE *(embracing the girls, a little too tightly)*: Ah, your beautiful daughters! Hello, everybody.

FATHER: Sit down, sit down. Girls, go help your mother.

>*(The girls go off to the side where their mother is, to help her, and to have fun, whispering "Mr. Levine is here!" Then pinching and fondling one another and laughing.)*

FATHER *(calling)*: Taube! Taube, where's the soup?

>*(Emma imitates him in whispers for Helena's benefit: "Taube, where's the soup!")*

FATHER: What are you talking about there, you two? Come and sit down like people.

>*(The girls bring the soup and sit at the far end of the table.)*

LEVINE: Mrs. Goldman, how are you liking Rochester?

FATHER *(answering for her)*: It's a thousand times better than New York.

EMMA *(carrying on her own whispering conversation with Helena at the end of the table)*: Our mother cannot speak for herself!

HELENA: Father knows her mind best! *(They've been through this before.)*

FATHER: Here, in Rochester, you see a flower, a blade of grass . . .

EMMA: One flower, one blade of grass . . .

>*(Helena giggles.)*

FATHER: It's not so crowded here as in New York . . .

EMMA: Only seven in one room . . .

FATHER *(sternly)*: No secrets there, girls! Be polite!

LEVINE: Was it hard finding work here?

FATHER: Oh, no, not hard at all.

>*(The girls are making faces like: "No, not hard at all!")*

FATHER *(turns to them, annoyed)*: What are you two making those noises for? Don't you know how to sit at a table? *(To Levine)* You know Jacob, Emma's husband. He has a good job. A big factory. They make beds.

EMMA *(speaking up this time)*: Six dollars a week. Twelve hours a day. He isn't home yet.

FATHER *(ignoring that)*: Emma has a job too. In the garment district. Emma, tell Mr. Levine about your job.

EMMA: What's to tell? The place stinks.

(Helena giggles.)

EMMA: Two dollars and fifty cents a week. We aren't allowed to sing. We aren't allowed to talk. The foreman tries to put his hands on the girls, so I have to give him a *zetz* in the face. *(She demonstrates; Helena giggles.)* Well *(shrugging)*, I'm not allowed to *talk* . . .

FATHER: What a mouth on her! She goes to these meetings, and she listens to these socialists, Communists, anarchists, who knows what they are? She doesn't realize what we all went through in the old country.

EMMA: I worked in a factory there too, Papa. It's no different, except here you have to work faster.

FATHER *(angrily)*: Here they don't kill Jews!

EMMA: They don't have to. The Jews kill themselves, on the machines.

FATHER: Here we have a place to live. Knock wood! *(Raps on the table)*

EMMA: Yes, wood. It burns fast. Last week, down the street, a whole family burned to death. You think that happens to Rockefeller in his stone mansion?

LEVINE: At least we have firemen here. Who knew from firemen in the old country?

EMMA: That's America. Here are the most firemen, and the most fires.

FATHER *(heatedly)*: We're lucky to be in Rochester. Where is it better, in New York? Packed into the tenements? The children dying of diphtheria, smallpox?

EMMA: At least, in New York, people are protesting. . . .

FATHER: All right! Go to New York, where all those *trumben-icks* are! Lazy slobs—they loaf around and then they scream

"America is no good." They don't appreciate this country.
(He bangs the table. Everyone is silent.)

MOTHER *(heading off an outburst)*: Emma, serve the soup.
(Emma starts serving.)

LEVINE *(trying to change the subject)*: I brought you the Yiddish
newspaper.

FATHER: Thanks, thanks. So, what's news?

LEVINE: You remember those fellows who threw the bomb in
Chicago last year and killed all those policemen?

EMMA *(loudly, firmly)*: No one ever found out who threw the
bomb. So they arrested eight anarchist organizers: a printer,
an upholsterer, a carpenter. . . .

FATHER: See—everything she knows. All right now, quiet
while Mr. Levine is talking.

LEVINE: I'm just telling what's in the paper. Yesterday, they
hanged four of them.
(Emma sobs. Helena puts her arm around her.)

FATHER: What are you crying for?

LEVINE: They were anarchists. They had it coming to them.

EMMA *(shouting)*: Shut up!

FATHER *(standing up, threatening)*: Respect!

LEVINE *(not wanting to make trouble, but needing to say something, shrugs)*: What's to cry about? They were murderers.

EMMA: Shut your mouth! *(She lifts a bowl of soup and throws it
into Mr. Levine's face.)*
*(Father starts after her, pulling at his belt. Her mother gets
between them.)*

MOTHER: She's upset! She's upset!

EMMA: You touch me and you'll get it right back!

FATHER *(enraged)*: What did you say?

EMMA: You heard me!

FATHER *(lifting the strap)*: I'll teach her.

MOTHER: Helena, take her away before her father kills her.

(Helena pulls Emma away. Mother hands Levine a towel to wipe his face.)

FATHER: That girl is crazy, out of her mind!

MOTHER: Shhhh! Shhhh!

(Lights down on the kitchen, then up again on Emma and Helena sitting on a cot in the corner, a faint light, music barely audible in the background, "Mein Ruhe Platz.")

EMMA: Sleep with me, Helena.

HELENA: Isn't Jacob going to sleep with you?

EMMA: We don't sleep together. Not since the first night. I should never have married him.

HELENA: Why did you?

EMMA: I was lonely.

HELENA: That's not a good reason.

EMMA: And stupid.

HELENA: *That's* a good reason.

EMMA: But no more. I have to live my own life. I've made up my mind. I'm going to New York.

HELENA: You're leaving Jacob, the family, your job?

EMMA: Everything.

HELENA: I wish I had your nerve.

EMMA: You like your husband. Why should you leave?

HELENA: If I had more nerve I wouldn't like him so much.

(They both laugh, then are quiet, then Helena starts to laugh again.)

EMMA: What's so funny?

HELENA: The soup! Did you see Papa's face?

EMMA: Did you see Mr. Levine's face?

(They both laugh. Then they are silent.)

EMMA: You know, Helena, I love you.

HELENA *(holding back tears)*: You take care of yourself in New

York. You heard what Papa said. That's where all the *trum-benicks* are!

(*They embrace, laughing, crying, as lights go down, music still faintly heard.*)

Scene Three

Sachs's Café. Lower Manhattan. A piano player. Mood of exuberance. Young people eating, drinking beer. Two tables. A hot August day. Mr. Sachs is playing the Italian game morra with the pianist between numbers, throwing fingers in the air, calling out. . . .

SACHS: Quattro! Due! Otto! Uno! . . .

(*Emma enters with Vito. She looks different, enjoying her freedom, at ease, although she is the stranger in this place. Vito is small, thin. He is smoking.*)

EMMA: It's wonderful here.

VITO: This is where we come after work. How many plans have been made here! How many revolutions have been won here!

(*Fedya sits at a table with Anna Minkin—she is smoking.*)

FEDYA: How much beer has been drunk here!

(*Emma and Vito laugh.*)

FEDYA: Sit down, Vito. Who is your friend?

(*Emma and Vito sit.*)

VITO (*calls out*): Mr. Sachs, two beers! This is Emma Goldman. She's just come from Rochester.

FEDYA: And before that?

EMMA: From Kovno, in Russia.

FEDYA: Ah . . . Kovno.

ANNA: He has no idea where it is. If you said "Schmetrogorsk,"
    Fedya would say: "Ah, Schmetrogorsk!"

FEDYA: So, you're from Rochester. I hear it's called the city of
    flowers.

EMMA: No, the city of flour, like in bread.

FEDYA: Welcome to New York, the city of sewers.

VITO: Fedya can't forget that I work in the sewers.

ANNA: Vito, you work in the sewers. But you're really a
    philosopher.

VITO: Is there a difference? But it's true. Everyone here is really
    something else. Anna works in a corset factory, but what
    is she really? An organizer of the corset workers. Fedya is
    unemployed. But what is he really? An artist.

FEDYA: Really, I'm unemployed.

EMMA: How is it, to work in the sewers?

VITO: First of all, it's temporary work. Just until there's a gen-
    eral constipation in New York.

    (Anna shakes her head—she knows Vito.)

VITO: According to the Marxian theory of capitalist crisis,
    the rich will get more and more constipated, and the poor
    will have less and less to eat, so the sewers will run dry. At
    which point I and my fellow sewer works, the true prole-
    tariat, will rise up *(He gets up dramatically.)* . . . out of the
    drek. . . .

SACHS: Enough! People are eating. . . .

VITO: There's no more to say. When that day comes, then you'll
    see something, Mr. Sachs.

SACHS: When you start paying for your beer, then we'll see
    something.

VITO: Don't worry, I get paid next Friday.

SACHS: My family has to eat *(holds up fingers)* Monday, Tuesday,
    Wednesday, Thursday . . .

VITO: And I don't have to eat?

SACHS: No, you're a revolutionary. You can live on hot air.

> *(Everyone laughs. Sachs resumes his game of morra with the pianist.)*

FEDYA: Laugh! When the Revolution comes, we'll collectivize this place, and then we'll have . . .

ANNA: Free beer!

> *(Everyone chants: "Free beer! Free beer!" Sachs goes off, shaking his head.)*

EMMA *(to Vito, smiling)*: So this is how anarchists in New York plan the revolution.

VITO: We work hard all day, and in the evening . . .

ANNA: Yes, during the day, in the shop, we denounce the capitalists. And in the evening, at Sachs Café, we denounce one another. There are the Marxists and the Bakuninists and the Kropotkinists and the DeLeonists . . .

EMMA: And you?

ANNA: Ah, when I first read Marx! *The Manifesto!* So clear, so glorious! *(She gets up on a chair.)* Workers of the world, unite! The capitalist system has created enormous wealth, but it has done this out of the misery of human beings. It is a sick system. How does it solve the problem of unemployment? By war and preparations for war. It must give way to a new society, where people share the work and share the wealth and live as human beings should. *(Everyone applauds; Anna bows.)* But then, I read Bakunin.

> *(Vito makes a gesture of disgust.)*

ANNA: At first, I hated him for his attacks on Marx. But I was intrigued. The dictatorship of the proletariat, he said, is like the dictatorship of the bourgeoisie. It will not wither away by itself. It will become a tyranny. There can be no workers' state. The state is an evil in itself. We must have no governments, no gods, no masters.

> *(Emma and Fedya applaud.)*

VITO: Bakunin is a dreamer, a romantic. Marx is rooted in history, in reality.

FEDYA: Three cheers for Bakunin!

VITO: Four cheers for Marx!

FEDYA *(holding up fingers in the morra spirit)*: Bakunin!

VITO: Marx!

ANNA *(laughing)*: Kropotkin!

VITO: Engels!

SACHS *(giving them all the finger)*: The revolution!

> *(A man comes into the café. Black hair, spectacles, strong face and jaw. He looks around, is clearly at home here.)*

VITO: Hello Sasha!

> *(Fedya and Anna too: "Hello Sasha." Sasha nods, sits down at a nearby table.)*

VITO *(to Emma)*: His name is Alexander Berkman. He never speaks until he eats.

SASHA *(calls to Sachs)*: Mr. Sachs. A steak, large. And a beer, large.

FEDYA: Sasha, who died and left you money?

SASHA: Today was payday.

VITO *(to Emma)*: He works in a cigar factory. Guess his age.

EMMA: Thirty-five?

VITO: Twenty-one.

EMMA: He's no older than me.

VITO: Sasha is older than everyone. *(He calls over.)* Hey, Sasha, say hello to our new comrade from Rochester, Emma Goldman.

SASHA *(looks up, nods, continuing to eat)*: Johann Most is speaking at the Academy of Music tomorrow night. *(He reaches into his package of rolled-up newspaper.)* I have the leaflets here.

EMMA: Johann Most himself?

SASHA *(looking up at her really for the first time)*: You've never heard him speak?

EMMA: No, but I read his articles in *Freiheit*.

SASHA *(nods, continuing to eat, looks up)*: Who will distribute on the West Side?

VITO *(to Emma)*: Sasha doesn't waste a moment. *(To Sasha)* Okay. I'll do the West Side on my lunch hour.

    (Sasha hands him a bunch of leaflets.)

ANNA: I'll do Union Square, right after work.

FEDYA: I'll help you. I'll see you there at six.

SASHA: I've got a shop meeting at lunch time. I'll distribute down on Broome Street an hour before I go to work.

ANNA: Sasha! You'll have to get up before five. . . .

SASHA: So?

ANNA: So nothing. After the revolution we will erect a statue right on Broome Street. *(She strikes a pose.)* Sasha—distributing leaflets before dawn.

EMMA: I have a room right near Broome Street. I'll help you.

SASHA: At five in the morning?

EMMA: If you'll be there, I'll be there.

VITO: Distributing leaflets with Sasha is an experience. *(He takes a bunch of leaflets, stands up, goes into his act, imitating Sasha on a street corner, speaking with gravity, as if addressing a passerby.)* "My good friend, do you realize that Johann Most is speaking tonight? Here is the information." *(Hands the leaflet to Fedya, then switches to the voice of the passerby.)* "Who? What? I have no time." *(Then back to Sasha's voice, with indignation)* "You have no time! Ten hours a day you give to the capitalists, and you can't spare one hour for the movement that will end your slavery? Shame on you!" *(He rams the leaflet into Fedya's stomach.)*

    (Fedya gasps. Everyone laughs. Sasha shakes his head, manages a smile: he can take it.)

VITO: Fedya distributing leaflets, that's another story. *(He assumes a gracious stance.)* "My dear madam, I have something for you. Do not fear. It is a free ticket to a concert. A concert of words. A symphony of ideas. The conductor? Johann Most. My pleasure, madam." *(He hands the leaflet to Emma, dances gracefully around her, humming a tune.)*

SASHA: Now let's be serious.

VITO: I'm serious, I'm serious. *(He pokes another leaflet into Fedya's stomach.)*

SASHA: I think it's not correct for Fedya and Anna to go to the same place and me and our friend Goldman to be at the same place. A waste of people. We could be covering more territory.

EMMA: No, it's not a waste. If a policeman comes along, it's harder for him to arrest two at once.

ANNA: She's right.

EMMA: Besides, it looks better to have two people. It shows we are an organization.

ANNA: She's right.

SASHA *(annoyed)*: She's *not* right. She's just come from Rochester, and she's telling us how to distribute leaflets in New York.

EMMA *(quietly)*: What a petty display of provincialism.

SASHA *(aggressively)*: What was that word?

EMMA: *Petty.*

SASHA: I mean the other word.

EMMA: Provincialism?

SASHA: I don't know that word.

(There is an embarrassed silence.)

EMMA *(softly):* You call yourself an anarchist.

SASHA *(angrily)*: Yes!

EMMA: And an internationalist?

SASHA: Of course!

EMMA: Provincialism is the opposite of internationalism.

SASHA: That's an insult!

ANNA: She's right, Sasha.

SASHA: "She's right, she's right"! Enough already!

VITO: Sasha, it's time you lost an argument.

EMMA: I'll meet you at five, Sasha. On Broome Street. Where the streetcar stops.

> *(She holds out her hand. Sasha looks at her curiously, slowly extends his hand. They shake hands, look at one another, the first trace of a smile in Sasha's eyes.)*

Scene Four

A revolutionary song, taped. The Deutschverein Hall, a spotlight on Johann Most, center stage, coat and tie, crew-cut hair, black-grey beard, tall, a distortion on the left side of his face from a childhood accident. He has force and dignity. He was a member of the German Reichstag. He has been imprisoned. He is a veteran of the revolutionary movement. A dramatic speaker, but able to slow down and almost whisper for effect. Here he is giving the audience a lesson in anarchism, as he is giving the police such a lesson. There is a policeman on each side of the stage, holding a club, in semi-darkness. It's a long speech for the stage, and can only work if Most grips the audience.

MOST: Comrades! Friends! And members of the New York City police. *(Laughter. Most peers into the audience, using his hand to shade his eyes. He points.)* Ah, there is Inspector Sullivan in the fourth row, taking notices. *(Laughter, applause)* Please, Inspector, get my name right—it's *Johann Most.* *(Most extends his hands, palms up. There is no longer a smile*

on his face. His tone is changing.) My friends, here we are, at
a peaceful meeting. There are women and children in the
audience. *(There is now anger in his voice.)* Yet the walls are
lined with police, carrying clubs, armed with guns. Is this
what is meant in America by freedom of speech?

(Murmurs in the audience)

MOST: Members of the police force, why are you here? Perhaps
you have heard that this is a meeting of anarchists. *(Laughter) Yes, we are anarchists! (Applause)* Perhaps you heard
that we believe in disorder. *(Claps his hands sharply together,
like a schoolmaster)* Wrong! We believe in *order.* No, not an
artificial order, enforced by the club and the gun, the courts
and the prisons, but the natural order of human beings
living and working together in equality, in harmony. Who
says we believe in chaos and disorder? The capitalists and
warmakers, the promoters of economic chaos, the archi-
tects of world disorder! *(Voice softens)* Let me explain to
you, Inspector Sullivan, and to you, members of the police
force, how we came to be anarchists. *(He pauses, stands very
erect.)* First, we examined our own lives and found we were
living by rules we had not made, in ways we did not want,
estranged from our most powerful human desires. Then,
we opened our eyes and looked around the city. At five in
the morning we could see the workers open their windows
to catch a breath of fresh air before going to the factory.
In the winter, we saw the corpses of old men and women
who froze because they had no fuel. In the summer we
saw the babies in the tenements dying of cholera. *(There
is total silence. His voice rises. His pace steps up.)* And we saw
something else. We saw that seven hundred buildings in
this city are owned by one family, the Astors, whose fortune
is one hundred million dollars. We saw that Jay Gould
had five hundred acres on the Hudson and a mansion on

Fifth Avenue, and that Rockefeller had taken control of
the nation's oil. Yes, we saw the rich living from the wealth
created by generations of workers. We saw that a party
was given at the Waldorf Astoria in honor of a dog. Yes, a
dog! Who was dressed in jewels, while mothers on Cherry
Street had no milk for their children. *(His voice is choked
with anger. He waits to get control and speaks more quietly.)*
We also saw that these same men who own the industries
of America pick the presidents and the congressmen. They
appoint the judges, anoint the priests, own the newspapers,
endow the universities.

> *(The police start smacking their clubs in their hands in
> unison. Most's voice rises above the sound.)*

MOST: Every year, thirty-five thousand workers die in *their*
mines and mills. Every generation, the sons of the workers are slaughtered in *their* wars. And they accuse us of
violence! *(He pauses, speaks very deliberately.)* Let us make
our position clear. Violence against innocent people? Never.
Violence against the oppressor? Always! *(Applause)* Yes,
take notes, Inspector Sullivan. We expect to hear from you.
(Laughter) But we are taking notes too. And some day, *some
day*, you will hear from us!

> *(Most bows, walks off to great applause, the stamping of
> feet, then the singing of the "Internationale" in German.
> The police are still smacking their clubs in their palms.)*
> *(Emma and Anna appear, as those sounds are still heard.
> They have been in the audience.)*

ANNA: What a meeting!

EMMA: So, that is Johann Most. I know now why he is in and
out of prison.

SASHA *(joining them)*: Hello Anna . . . Hello Emma.

> *(Fedya joins them too. He is wearing a finely embroidered
> shirt. Sasha shakes his head.)*

SASHA: Look at that shirt. You can always tell an artist.

FEDYA: Sasha is annoyed by my shirt.

EMMA: I think it's beautiful.

SASHA: We all have our tastes. But should we spend money on such things when the movement needs every cent we have?

EMMA: Don't we need beautiful things to remind us of what life can be like some day?

SASHA: Should an anarchist enjoy luxuries while people live in poverty?

ANNA: When Jews talk, everyone asks questions. No one gives answers.

EMMA: Must we give up music and the smell of lilacs to be revolutionaries?

ANNA *(nudging Fedya)*: See?

SASHA: Who said you have to give up music or flowers? But shirts like this, yes.

FEDYA: What about art?

SASHA: It's an objective fact: the artist lives on the backs of the poor. Don't take it personally, Fedya.

FEDYA: Why shouldn't I? Am I not a person?

EMMA: Sasha, there is something wrong with the way you think. I can't quite express it. . . .

SASHA: If you were right, you would be able to express it.

EMMA *(calmly)*: You are insufferable.

SASHA *(good-humoredly)*: I don't know what that means, but I think I have been insulted again.

ANNA: I think, Sasha, it means you want us all to suffer until the revolution comes.

SASHA: You don't understand.

ANNA: I understand, and I'm going home right now—to suffer! Are you coming, Emma?

EMMA: I'll come a little later. I want to change the dates on these posters. Most is speaking again in two weeks.

ANNA *(to the men)*: She's staying with me until she finds
a job. *(She starts to leave, nudges Fedya until he begins to
comprehend.)*

FEDYA *(simulating a yawn)*: I'm tired. I'll walk home with you
Anna. *(They go off.)*

SASHA *(watching Fedya leave, shaking his head)*: He's tired!
He sleeps all morning. *(Hesitates, his voice softens as he turns
to Emma.)* How about a little walk?

EMMA: I'm not finished with these posters yet.

SASHA: And let's not argue. After all, we're comrades.

EMMA: Shouldn't comrades argue?

SASHA: Now she wants to argue about arguing! *(They are silent
as she continues to work on the posters.)* Let's go for a seltzer.

EMMA *(having fun)*: Isn't that a luxury?

SASHA *(after a pause)*: A plain seltzer?

EMMA: What if I want a little chocolate syrup in it?

SASHA *(entering into the spirit)*: I'm not as dogmatic as you
think. A *little* chocolate syrup.

EMMA *(her tone changes)*: How did you come to be what you are,
Sasha?

SASHA: You mean, insufferable?

EMMA: Yes. No. I mean, your ideas. Our ideas. They tell me
you're organizing the cigar workers.

SASHA: In the old country, at the age of thirteen, I was expelled
from school for writing an essay.

EMMA: For an essay?

SASHA: The title was considered somewhat tactless. "There Is
No God."

(They laugh.)

EMMA: At thirteen, I was already working in a factory in
St. Petersburg. I did not know words like capitalism, anti-
Semitism, the State. But it was all so clear. Who needs the
words, when you feel it in your bones every day?

SASHA: Didn't you think America would be different?

EMMA: In the factory in Rochester, I could feel no difference.
Yes, America had a Constitution. But it meant nothing in
the factory.

SASHA: It meant nothing for those executed after Haymarket.

EMMA: So many of us had our eyes opened by Haymarket.

SASHA: I'll never forget the last words of Spies to the jury:
"These are my ideas. They constitute a part of myself. I
cannot divest myself of them, nor would I if I could. . . .
I say, if death is the penalty for proclaiming the truth,
call your hangman."

(Both are moved at hearing those words again.)

SASHA: I hope I will have such courage when the time comes.

EMMA *(coming closer, grasping his hands)*: Sasha! You're too
young to talk of dying.

SASHA: One day, the choice will be before us, to bow down,
or to risk all. To give our lives, if necessary.

EMMA: I am ready to give my life for what I believe in. But I
would like to give it over a period of fifty years, not in one
heroic moment. The movement needs us to live for it, not
to die for it.

SASHA: Perhaps only our grandchildren will be able to live full
lives.

EMMA: I don't believe that. We must live ourselves. And
beautifully, to show how life can be lived. *(In her fervor,
she has held onto his hands, come closer to him. They are suddenly conscious of their closeness and break away.)*

SASHA *(hesitates)*: What are you doing tomorrow?

EMMA: I have to go to the baggage room at Grand Central. I
left my sewing machine there.

SASHA: You brought it all the way from Rochester?

EMMA: Yes, I'm tired of working in a corset factory. I'd like to work for myself, maybe set up a cooperative shop. Like Vera in *What Is to Be Done?*

SASHA: Oh, have you read Chernishevsky?

EMMA: Why are you surprised?

SASHA: Well, you're so young.

EMMA: So are you.

SASHA: But I am a man.

EMMA *(her anger rising)*: And I am a woman.

SASHA: You are very sensitive

EMMA: And *you* are very *insensitive.*

SASHA *(sighing)*: Do you think you and I will ever be good friends?

EMMA *(softly)*: Aren't we? *(A second of silence)* Sasha, let's go for that seltzer some other time. Anna is waiting and she needs her sleep.

SASHA: All right! Tomorrow I'll come with you to Grand Central. I know my way around the city. Afterward, if you like, we can take the El down to the Brooklyn Bridge and walk across. The air is wonderful on the river.

EMMA *(incredulous)*: I didn't ask you to come with me! Don't you have to work?

SASHA *(a little abashed)*: This morning, when I went to work, I made a tactical mistake. I gave some of our leaflets to the workers. The foreman said: "This is your last day." So, I'll come for you tomorrow.

(Emma starts to respond. He holds up his hand.)

SASHA: I know where Anna Minkin lives. What time?

(Emma doesn't respond.)

SASHA: What time?

EMMA: Ten o'clock.

SASHA: Good. Before I meet you, I can look for a job.

EMMA: I saw how much you eat. You need a job.

SASHA: Emma . . . I think you are . . . insufferable. *(He turns to go, then turns back.)*

> *(They both smile. He turns again and goes.)*

Scene Five

Anna Minkin's apartment. Flute music. Emma and Sasha tiptoe into the apartment. It is dark and quiet. She is wearing a sailor hat.

EMMA: Come in, we can talk a while.

SASHA: Will we wake up Anna?

EMMA: Nothing can wake up Anna. *(To prove it, she stamps on the floor, then listens. No reaction)* You see? *(They slowly embrace in the dark.)*

ANNA *(from the other room, sleepily)*: For God's sake, a little quiet!

> *(Emma and Sasha break off, listen. Emma shrugs. It is quiet again. They slowly embrace once more, and kiss, the music still soft in the background as the scene ends.)*

Scene Six

Anna's apartment. Lively piano music, exuberant, befitting a scene of four young, attractive, life-loving, dedicated people. Emma and Sasha are sitting, having tea in glasses. Sasha is enjoying it, blowing, cooling, sipping. Anna and Fedya enter.

SASHA: Look, he's wearing that shirt again!

EMMA *(to Sasha, softly)*: Who's going to tell Anna, you or me?

SASHA: I'll tell her.

ANNA: Tell what?

EMMA: That girl hears everything.

ANNA: Yes, *everything. (Laughs, bends to kiss Emma)*

EMMA: Anna dear, Toby Golden is moving out of her place on Forsyth Street. It's five dollars a month. Sasha and I are going to take it.

ANNA *(teasing)*: So, you'd rather live with Sasha than with me. A true friend!

EMMA: Anna, you know this place is just big enough for you. With me here you've had no privacy at all.

ANNA: You mean ever since Sasha started coming around. *(She dances around provocatively, groaning and sighing.)* It's been *oy* and *ah,* and *ooh* and *mmmm.* Yes *(embraces Emma),* you need a place. I know Toby Golden's place. It's twice as big as this apartment, isn't it?

SASHA: Yes, twice as big.

ANNA: Good! Then there's room for me.

SASHA: Now look, Anna . . .

ANNA: Do you believe in collectivity or not?

SASHA: Of course, but . . .

ANNA *(orating, imitating Sasha, or someone)*: Bourgeois individualism corrupts us all! We must begin the new culture right now, comrades! Share and share alike! Break through the prison of monogamy!

EMMA: Of course, she's right, Sasha.

SASHA *(gloomily)*: Of course she's right.

FEDYA *(has been walking around, rearranging pictures on the walls, now stops)*: I know Toby Golden's place. There are three big rooms.

ANNA: Yes, you see?

FEDYA: Yes, it's big enough for me too.

ANNA: You too?

FEDYA *(jumping onto the bed, imitating Anna)*: We must begin the new culture now, comrades. Love thy neighbor, says the Bible. Workers of the world unite, says Marx. Live in free association, says Kropotkin. Make room for Fedya, says Fedya!

ANNA: Fedya, I'm not the same with you as Emma with Sasha. We're just friends.

FEDYA: Yes, and we'll live together as friends. What do we always say? *(He orates again.)* Between men and women there must be an endless variety of relationships—passion, companionship . . .

ANNA: Hostility! Murder! *(She playfully attacks him.)*

EMMA *(excited)*: The four of us together! It *is* big enough. There's a bedroom, and we can put a bed in the living room and a folding bed in the kitchen.

SASHA *(he has been gloomy in a corner. Now he is aroused)*: Why stop with four? How about a bed in the bathroom too? Then my friend Yussel Miller can join us. We could put the bed upright and Yussel can sleep standing up. *(He is a little bitter.)*

EMMA *(disapprovingly)*: Sasha!

SASHA: Don't say another word. *(He comes over to them, puts his arms around them.)* You are right. You are all right. When I'm wrong I admit it. We're all friends and comrades. Why can't we live together, live collectively? That's the way of the future. And we have to start the future now. *(But he doesn't look too happy.)*

ANNA *(jumping up)*: Yes! Yes!

FEDYA *(producing a bottle of wine he had wrapped in a newspaper)*: Let's drink to our little collective.

SASHA *(shaking his head)*: Every time you see him he has a bottle of wine.

FEDYA *(uncorking it with a loud noise right in front of Sasha)*: Emma, you wash some glasses, I'll pour the wine.
(Emma shrugs and goes to do it.)

SASHA: We'll all contribute equally to the rent and food.

EMMA: We'll all contribute according to our ability. Anna and I are working in the corset shop. You're working in a cigar factory.

SASHA: And Fedya can sell his shirt. We can live on that for a month.

ANNA: Don't laugh. When Fedya sells a painting, he makes more than I can make in a week.

SASHA: Fedya, when's the last time you sold a painting?

FEDYA: What day is it?

ANNA: Wednesday.

FEDYA *(counting on his fingers)*: About a year ago . . .

SASHA: Well, I can see we will eat well.

FEDYA: None of us will eat as well as you, Sasha. You eat and drink as much as the three of us.

EMMA: To each according to his need. Sasha needs to eat like a horse. Fedya needs to sleep late in the morning. I need to read without people talking to me. And Anna *(turns her head mischievously)* . . . Anna needs to spend about an hour in the toilet every morning.

ANNA: A perfect group! We'll never interfere with one another. Fedya will be sleeping. Sasha will be eating. Emma will be reading. And I'll be in the toilet. *(She takes their hands to execute a little place-changing routine.)* And every hour, we can change places.

FEDYA: Let's drink to our needs!
(Emma pours wine for all of them. Sasha slugs it down with great enjoyment.)

SASHA: We can organize the tenants in Toby's building.

EMMA: Oh, what the four of us can do together!

(Fedya pours the wine for all of them. Again Sasha drinks it down in a gulp and Fedya pours him another. Anna starts singing a Yiddish tune—"Mein Greeneh Kuzine." She takes Emma's hand and they dance. Then Emma takes Fedya's hand and the three of them dance.)

EMMA: Come on, Sasha!

SASHA: Each to his need. I'll have more wine. *(He pours himself another glass as the others spin around him. But then he starts dancing himself.)* To tell you the truth, I think I'm a little drunk! *(He is smiling happily, suddenly calls out.)* Fedya, I want your shirt!

(Fedya flamboyantly takes off his shirt, throws it at Sasha. Sasha holds it over his head, dancing. All four dance exuberantly as the music quickens to "Mein Greeneh Kuzine.")

Scene Seven

Fedya is sketching on the kitchen table. He looks up in surprise. Emma has just come in, weary. She puts down her workbag.

EMMA: It's so hot up here, Fedya. How can you work? It's worse than the shop.

FEDYA: You're home so early. Is something wrong?

EMMA: Kargman found out who is organizing the union. Three of us were fired this morning. It was a big commotion. More girls wanted to walk out, but we told them to wait. After work today, they'll be a meeting, and if enough girls come . . . Well, we'll see. . . . Oh God, it's so hot. *(She removes her shirt, is wearing a camisole.)*

FEDYA: Emma, what are you doing?

EMMA *(amused)*: Fedya, darling, you've seen me like this before.

FEDYA: Yes, with everybody here. But like this . . .

EMMA: I'll put my blouse back on, if it makes you nervous.

FEDYA: Why should I be nervous? After all, I'm an artist. At the Settlement House, we painted nude figures all the time. We had models. Now I can't afford that. I paint nudes from memory. *(He smiles.)* And my memory is not too good.

EMMA: If you ever want me to pose for you, Fedya, just tell me.

FEDYA: You're serious, Emma?

EMMA: Why not? We're friends and comrades. *(She leans over and kisses him on the cheek.)*

(He gets up and paces the floor nervously.)

EMMA: What's the matter?

FEDYA: I would like you to pose for me, Emma. But I don't know. . . .

EMMA: What is it?

FEDYA *(stops pacing, comes over to her)*: I have been so troubled. *(Shakes his head)* Sasha is my friend, and yet . . . I have been longing for you, Emma. I have, yes. I can't help it. . . . *(He takes her hand.)*

EMMA *(she strokes his hair)*: Sweet Fedya. It's all right. It's all right. We both love Sasha. But Sasha and I don't own one another. Why shouldn't you have feelings for me? Why shouldn't I have feelings for you?

FEDYA *(taking both her hands)*: Emma . . . do you think . . . ?

EMMA: Why are we living? Why are we struggling and organizing? What is this all for? Sometimes, in the midst of all the turmoil, I forget, and I have to remind myself, and then I think of the very first time I realized that life could be . . . ecstatic. It was back in the old country. I must have been eight or nine. This peasant boy worked around the farm, and one day he took me out in the meadow. The sun was strong. We sat in the long grass and he played his flute. Then he lifted me in his arms and threw me into the air and caught me. Everything smelled of grass. My soul melted. He caught me again and again.

(Fedya presses his lips to her hair.)

EMMA: Years after that, I was with my aunt in Konigsberg. She took me to the opera. *Il Trovatore.* Such golden voices. Such heavenly music. I had never in my life been to any theater—I sat there in the balcony as in a trance. When it was over, I heard the crash of applause. Everyone was leaving, and my aunt was calling me, but I sat there in my seat, the tears streaming down my face. . . . When we sailed for America, out of my old life almost everything was forgotten, but on the boat I thought of the peasant boy on the farm, and the Opera House in Konigsberg. I was young. I knew so little, but at that moment I knew what I wanted life to be. . . .

(She throws her arms around Fedya, and he around her, in a long embrace. He sits up, shakes his head in confusion.)

EMMA: What's the matter?

FEDYA: I am Sasha's friend.

EMMA: That makes it better.

FEDYA: I feel like a betrayer.

EMMA: You've taken nothing from him. He and I are still as we were.

FEDYA: Will he see it that way?

EMMA: You know Sasha. At first he will be angry.

FEDYA: Oh, will he be angry!

EMMA: He may smash a piece of furniture.

FEDYA: Maybe two or three.

EMMA: And then he'll say . . .

FEDYA *(orating like Sasha)*: I was wrong—when I'm wrong I admit it. We must live like free people—we must live as in the future society.

EMMA: Yes, that's exactly what he will say.

FEDYA: I love Sasha. . . .

> *(Music as scene ends.)*

Scene Eight

Kargman's. Picket line, including Emma and Anna, with signs, walking, shouting. One picket has a bandaged head. A policeman stands by, holding a club.

PICKETERS: Strike! Strike! Stay out! Don't work for Kargman, stay out! Strike! Strike! Don't work for Kargman, stay out!

> *(A striker comes running up to the line, excited. . . .)*

STRIKER: Scabs! They're bringing scabs!

> *(A small group of girls, women, led by a well-dressed man, arrive. The striker who just spoke picks up a rock. Emma puts a hand on his arm.)*

EMMA: No, Yankele, wait.

> *(The pickets mass in front of the shop entrance. The scabs stop.)*

EMMA: Look at them. They're just off the boat. Look at their faces. They're hungry, just like us!

> *(Yankele moves back. The scab leader rushes forward, knocking Emma down. Her friends rush back. The policeman moves in, lifts his club threateningly, they move back to the line. Emma walks back and forth quickly around the scabs, speaking to them.)*

EMMA: *Schwester! Bruder! Herr zu!* Listen to me! They didn't tell you there's a strike here, and you are taking our jobs.

> *(The man leading the scabs comes up to her threateningly, grabs her arm.)*

MAN: Get the hell away from here before I break your head!

> (*Emma pulls her arm away angrily. The other strikers have come off the line to her side.*)

EMMA: Keep walking comrades! (*She keeps walking herself, continuing to speak to the scabs, then stops as someone puts a box before her. She mounts it, at first hesitantly, then lifts her head and addresses the scabs directly, appealingly.*) I know you need to work. Your families are hungry. *Azoi wie unsere.* Just like ours! Your houses are cold. *Azoi wie unsere!* Just like ours. Kargman has promised you good wages. But let me tell you something, brothers and sisters. We know Kargman well. He is a liar! *Er iz ah ligner!* But you know that already, because he didn't tell you there was a strike here! He despises you, just as he despises us. *Er iz dein Sonne!* He is your enemy! Just as he is ours. He will pay you good wages, yes, until the strike is over. But what happens then? Then he will cut your wages, as he cut ours. And you'll go on strike, just like us. And the police will come and smash you with their clubs, just as they do to us! And then Kargman will get others to take your place.

> (*The policeman moves toward her, raises his club. Emma raises her picket stick, he steps back.*)

EMMA: Brothers, sisters! (*She is gaining confidence. This is her first speech.*)

> (*The well-dressed man calls to the scabs: "Come on, let's go in!" He starts pushing forward. The scabs seem uncertain.*)

EMMA (*speaking with great strength now*): Schwester! Bruder!

> (*The power, urgency in her voice make them turn.*)

EMMA: If you try to go in there'll be a fight. We shouldn't fight one another. Together we can make our lives better. Listen. We are not alone! All over the country, working people like us are joining together. Right now, in Pennsylvania, three thousand workers are saying "Enough!" to the richest man in America, Andrew Carnegie. Enough to working twelve hours a day in the steel furnaces! Enough to a heat like in hell! Enough to fourteen cents an hour! Enough! Three thousand workers standing together, refusing to scab on one another. . . . Let us stand together too! Join us, my brothers and sisters. *(Almost a whisper now)* Don't work for Kargman!

> *(They seem frozen in place by her words. The well-dressed man is shouting at them: "Inside! Inside!" But they don't move. Then one of then, a women, shawl on her head, comes forward to Emma. She is weeping. She holds out her hands. Emma grasps them. The picket line continues chanting.)*

PICKETERS: Stay out! Stay out! Don't work for Kargman! Strike! Strike!

Scene Nine

Music, from Bizet's Carmen. *Sasha is sitting at the kitchen table, writing intently. Emma comes in from outside, flushed, holding violets, humming from the opera music. She puts an arm around Sasha gaily, kisses him on the cheek.*

EMMA: Oh, what a picket line at Kargman's today!

SASHA *(without looking up, continuing to write)*: Anna told me. You made your first speech. She said it was good. . . . *(He looks up.)* You've been away all evening.

EMMA: Yes. *(She hums.)*

> *(Sasha does not respond, continues working.)*

EMMA: Sasha dear, what are you doing up so late?

SASHA *(without looking up)*: A leaflet on the strike in Pittsburgh. Have you heard the latest news?

EMMA: No.

SASHA: Carnegie has put Frick in charge. You know him. Henry Clay Frick. A lover of art. A gangster. And Frick has called in the Pinkertons. You know them. The biggest strike-breaking agency in America. Two thousand men, with the latest weapons.

EMMA: A private army . . .

SASHA: And Frick is going to use them to break the strike. The strikers will need money, weapons, support from all over the country, or they are done for. I must finish this leaflet tonight. *(He looks up at Emma.)* Where have you been all evening?

EMMA: Johann invited me to go to the Metropolitan Opera House with him. We saw *Carmen*.

SASHA: Johann? *(His temper is rising.)* Johann who?

EMMA: Johann Most.

SASHA: So now it's *Johann*! The opera! That's how Most uses the movement's money. *(Thinks)* The opera must have ended hours ago.

EMMA: We went to a restaurant afterward.

SASHA: A restaurant! You probably drank wine all evening too.

EMMA *(heatedly)*: Yes, we drank wine!

SASHA: Of course. Most loves expensive wine. That's our great revolutionary leader.

EMMA: Most is a wonderful man. You told me so yourself. He gave up his seat in the German Reichstag. He became an anarchist. He spent years in prison. He risked his life!

SASHA *(coldly)*: The Movement gives no special benefits for war veterans. The most heroic figures can become corrupt. We see that in history.

EMMA: Then I am corrupt too, by going to the opera, by drinking wine?

SASHA: Yes! You too! You're worse than Most, you with your

pretensions, cuddling up to every leader of the movement. . . .

EMMA: Shut your mouth!

SASHA: I'm speaking the truth and you know it. What are you
holding there?

EMMA *(defiantly)*: They're violets. Yes, I know flowers are an
unnecessary expense when people are starving. Well, they
are beautiful and I love them. *(She puts them in a jar.)*

SASHA: It makes me nauseous to see them when the strikers
in Pittsburgh are in need of bread.

EMMA *(angered and hurt)*: And what are *you* doing about the
families in Pittsburgh? Writing a leaflet!

SASHA: Yes, we need to write leaflets.

EMMA: It will take more than that.

SASHA *(shouting)*: And I'm prepared to do more than that.

EMMA: So am I. And so is Most.

SASHA: We will see.

EMMA: What do you mean?

SASHA: We will see.

EMMA *(more softly)*: Don't you understand, Sasha? We can't all
live at the level of the most oppressed. We have to have a
little beauty in our lives, even in the midst of struggle.

SASHA: You think Most cares about beauty? What do you think
was in Most's mind when he gave you those violets?

EMMA: You're jealous, Sasha. I thought you had overcome that.
I thought you believed in my freedom.

SASHA: Freedom, yes! Decadence, no! With Fedya it is different. Fedya, we both love. But Most! He is not good for you,
Emma.

EMMA *(angrily)*: Who is to decide that, you or me?

SASHA *(a little subdued)*: Yes, that's for you to decide. *(Suddenly
angry at her scoring a point, he bangs his fist on the table.)*

ANNA *(emerging from her room in her nightgown)*: Will you two stop that? You've kept me up for the past half hour. I've got to be on the picket line early in the morning. You do too, Emma.

(Another voice from the next apartment: "Shut up in there!" Some banging on the walls, general protest over loss of sleep. Someone yells "Quiet already!")

EMMA: Yes, for God's sake, let's go to sleep.

ANNA *(turning on her)*: You don't care. None of you care anymore—you and Sasha and Fedya—you're moving to Wor-chester, Massachusetts, so you don't give a damn about anybody.

EMMA *(correcting her)*: Wooster.

ANNA *(rejecting the correction)*: To Wor-chester. And without me.

EMMA: You said you wanted to have nothing to do with our idea.

ANNA: Such a brilliant idea. An ice cream parlor run by revolutionaries. What kind of revolution will you have today, sir? Vanilla? Chocolate? Not strawberry! Not a real *red* revolution. Not in a petty-bourgeois ice cream parlor?

EMMA: It's just for a little while, Anna. We need the money to start our new magazine.

ANNA: The three of you are leaving me here alone. *(Her voice is breaking.)*

SASHA: You wanted to stay, Anna.

ANNA: I didn't want to go to Wor-chester. *(She bursts out crying. Emma comforts her.)*

EMMA *(wearily)*: Why are we all fighting? Let's go to sleep.

(Voices from the other apartment, shouting: "Go to sleep, you bums!")

SASHA *(replying)*: Go to hell, all of you!

ANNA: You wanted to organize them, now you curse them.

SASHA: Oh, shut up and go back to sleep.

ANNA *(to Emma)*: How can you put up with that man?
> *(She starts to leave.)*
>> *(Fedya arrives.)*

FEDYA: What's all this noise?

EMMA: Go to sleep!

FEDYA: I'll go to sleep when I feel like! *(He returns now to his usual low-key demeanor.)* Did you hear about Pittsburgh?
> *(Anna turns back to listen.)*

EMMA: Sasha told me. The Pinkertons have been called in.

FEDYA: Well, they started. There was a battle there today.

SASHA: Today?

FEDYA: Frick brought a hundred Pinkertons down the river on a barge. An army of them. Machine guns, rifles. They opened fire on men, women, children. There are seven dead.
> *(Emma puts her hands to her head as if to shut out the news.)*

SASHA *(looking at Emma, with combined anguish and fury)*: While you were at the opera! *(He smashes the vase of violets with a sweep of his hands.)*

EMMA *(shouting, weeping)*: While you were writing a damn leaflet! Don't talk to me that way, you bastard!

FEDYA: Stop it, you two. What are we going to do?

SASHA *(to himself, pacing the floor, fists clenched)*: What's wrong with me? I must be crazy! Going with you two to Massachusetts to open an ice cream parlor so we can publish some intellectual garbage! I must be out of my mind. I should be in Pittsburgh right now, with the strikers.

EMMA: And what are you going to do in Pittsburgh?

SASHA: It was you who said: "It will take more than leaflets. . . ."

EMMA: Yes, I said it, but . . .

SASHA: But! But! There is something that must be done in Pittsburgh. *(He is speaking calmly, thoughtfully now. The others watch him as he paces the floor, building up his rationale and his resolve at the same time.)* We must show the world that the Carnegies, the Rockefellers, the Fricks are not invincible. We see their pictures in the newspapers. The arrogance in their faces. The contempt in their eyes for all who have not succeeded in their game of becoming rich. Yes, the pictures. Frick going to church. Frick in the White House with the president, while his workers fall from exhaustion in the mills. Frick, drinking whiskey at his country club while his detectives shoot down women and children. Frick. Yes, there is something that must be done in Pittsburgh.

FEDYA: What are you talking about?

SASHA: Frick must die.

EMMA: Keep your voice down. Are you crazy?

SASHA: What does your friend Most say? "There are times in history when a bullet speaks louder than a thousand manifestos."

EMMA: Yes. Yes. *(She is thinking desperately, not sure of what to do and speaks almost to herself.)* We have all said to one another, that when the right time came . . .

FEDYA *(excited)*: We would be ready! Yes, we said that. We all did. *(There is anguish in his voice now as it all becomes more real.)*

SASHA: I'm going to Pittsburgh. . . .

EMMA: We'll all go. It is the right moment. All through the centuries they have slaughtered the working people. They are never punished. And now once more. But this time, it will be different. We will show everyone—they can die too!

ANNA *(trembling)*: The four of us can do it.

FEDYA: It will have to be planned very carefully. *(He is nervous.)*

EMMA: But it will go around the world. It is the right time. We can do it.

SASHA *(quietly)*: Who kills Frick surrenders his life.

EMMA *(crying out)*: We said we are ready. Remember how the

four of us said we are ready? How we would stand together when the time came?

SASHA: I will do it alone. *(A second of silence, astonishment)*

EMMA: You are crazy, Sasha!

SASHA: No, we will not give them four lives for one. No.

EMMA: You're not going to do it yourself!

FEDYA: What are we talking about? It takes money to go to Pittsburgh. And what will it be? A bomb? A gun? It takes money.

SASHA: That's right. And we don't have the train fare for one.

EMMA: If we can raise the money for one, we can do it for four. I will get the money somehow.

SASHA *(shaking his head slowly, firmly)*: It's not the money.

EMMA *(almost screaming, but trying to keep her voice down)*: Well, what is it then? You want to do it all by yourself? You want to say, to hell with our comradeship, our love? Is that it?

SASHA: You won't understand. If Frick is killed, someone must explain. Someone must know why it was done, and explain. Otherwise they will say, as they always do, it was the work of a madman.

FEDYA: They will say it anyway.

SASHA: No, Emma can explain it. She has the tongue. She has the gift. She can do it. All of you must stay behind and make it clear to the whole country, to the world.

FEDYA *(almost in tears)*: But I'm not needed for that. I'm no speaker. I can help you, Sasha. Together . . .

SASHA *(shouting)*: No! *(The word comes like an explosion.)* Fedya, we don't have to sacrifice you too.

EMMA: Keep your voices down. *(She is in despair.)*

SASHA: You know I'm right. You know it's necessary. A moment comes when someone must act, must point, must say: "Enough!" You know that. . . .

EMMA *(almost whispering)*: Yes, Sasha . . .

SASHA *(very calm now)*: All right . . . money. A train ticket. A device that will kill . . .

EMMA *(becoming calm now, holding back her feelings)*: You will need a new suit of clothes. . . .

ANNA *(almost in tears)*: Yes . . .

SASHA *(totally calm)*: Let's sit down and make plans.

> *(With a sudden gesture he embraces Fedya, Anna, Emma. They hold him tightly. Then, almost in slow motion, they sit down at the table as the lights go down to end the scene.)*

Scene Ten

In the darkness, a steady drumbeat. Then an eerie light on the scene, which will take place in semi-darkness. Frick and another man are sitting, talking, on one side of the stage, while Sasha can be seen on the other side, in the shadows, getting dressed in his new suit.

MAN: Is that the American way, to riot in the street when things don't go right?

FRICK: We don't riot when things don't go right. We go through the proper channels.

MAN: We go to the Speaker of the House.

FRICK: We go to the Attorney General.

MAN: We go to the Secretary of the Treasury.

FRICK: And they always respond to us with generosity.

MAN: That is democracy. . . .

> *(Sasha stands up, fully dressed, faces the Frick office.)*

SECRETARY *(off)*: Do you have an appointment? Mr. Frick cannot see you now. You must see Miss O'Neil.

MISS O'NEIL *(off)*: I'm sorry, but Mr. Frick cannot see you now. *(Her voice rises.)* Where are you going?

SASHA *(walking toward Frick, calls out)*: Frick!

(Frick rises from his chair. Sasha fires, misses. Pandemonium. Sasha is pounced upon by two men who have run into the office. He breaks loose, goes at Frick with a knife, stabs, is knocked down, bodies over him. You see an arm with a hammer rising and falling. Sasha is groaning. Then silence, darkness.)

SASHA *(off)* *(his voice is weak, delirious with pain, almost a whisper)*: My glasses! Where are my glasses? I can't see. . . . I can't see. . . .

Act Two | Prologue

TAPED VOICE: Alexander Berkman, for the attempted murder of Henry Clay Frick, you are sentenced to the Western Pennsylvania State Penitentiary for a period of twenty-two years. *(Rapping of a gavel)*

EMMA *(Standing in the shadows, as if watching the scene from five hundred miles away, cries out in anguish)*: Sa-sha-a-a!

Scene One

Lights up on Johann Most, center stage, hand extended toward the audience. The beat of a revolutionary song in the background, in German.

MOST: Comrades, some here are circulating petitions for Alexander Berkman. I have refused to sign. Let me explain: revolutionary violence is one thing—a comic opera is another. *(Applause. Most holds up his hand. He is serious. His humor is biting. He doesn't mind if people laugh, but his intent is serious. He doesn't smile.)* Comrades! I am not urging anyone here to assassinate the nearest capitalist—well, not publicly. *(Laughter and applause)* But let me say this: if you

do decide on it, please do it efficiently. *(Laughter)* They
tell me that before the shooting, Berkman made a bomb
to kill Frick. There was only one thing wrong with Berkman's bomb—it would not explode! *(More laughter)* Now
comrades, I'm not urging the making of bombs—no, never!
(He is ironic—everyone knows he has urged making bombs.)
But it seems to me there is one essential requirement for a
bomb. It should explode! I understand Berkman's trade is
cigar-making. Maybe he thought it was like making a cigar.
(Laughter) Well all right, his cigar—I mean, his bomb—
did not work. So he fired his gun. Comrades, one piece of
advice: if you fire a gun at a capitalist, don't close your eyes!
(Laughter, applause) When his shots missed, he took out his
knife. Now we must admire one thing about Berkman—
he was well armed! *(More laughter)* But what he really
needed was a guillotine, an agreement from Frick to hold
his head still . . .

> *(A woman has stood up in the audience, not immediately
> recognizable because she is in the front row, facing Most,
> or on the aisle.)*

MOST: Comrades *(getting serious now, emphasizing each word)*,
we have a revolution to make and we will have to do it right!
So don't come to me *(showing anger)* with petitions for
that fool, Alexander Berkman! *(Applause. The woman is still
standing. Most peers into the audience to see who it is. Then,
graciously . . .)* Comrades, I recognize Emma Goldman, who
is known to you as an organizer of the cloak and suit workers. I believe she has a question. . . .

EMMA *(her voice strong and clear)*: I have no question. *(She just
stands there.)*

MOST *(trying to maintain the appearance of good humor)*: No
question?

EMMA *(loudly)*: Shame on you, Johann Most!

MOST *(straining for humor)*: That is not a question. . . .

EMMA *(her voice shaking with anger)*: Shame, shame on you!

> *(She leaps onto the stage and stands facing Most.)*
>> *(He is angry, rattled.)*

MOST: Do you have a question?

EMMA *(dressed in a long cloak, she pulls a whip from under her cloak and, as she strikes Most with it, cries out)*: Shame!

>> *(Most falls back, covers his face. Four more strokes with the whip)*

EMMA: Shame! Shame! Shame! Shame!!

>> *(Several men jump on stage to stop her. She flings the whip at Most, then turns to the audience, standing straight.)*

EMMA *(in a low, emotional voice)*: Shame on all of you!

Scene Two

Ragtime music. Fedya and Emma on a station platform. She is carrying a suitcase, wearing a hat, look quite respectable.

EMMA: How good of you to wait with me, Fedya dear. I know how busy you are these days with your art.

FEDYA: A lucky chance that I have an exhibition in the same city where you are giving a lecture. It's been so long since . . .

EMMA: Yes. *(She grasps his hand.)*

FEDYA: Who is meeting you?

EMMA: A Dr. Reitman. I don't know anything about him.

>> *(A man has been standing on the opposite side of the stage, dark hair falling over his eyes, tall, with a mustache, wearing a silk tie and a big hat, carrying a cane. A confident man)*

EMMA *(glancing over, amused)*: Is that how men dress in Chicago?

FEDYA: A bit odd. But handsome, no?

EMMA: Handsome, yes. But a bit odd.
(The man is walking toward them.)

FEDYA *(whispering)*: I think . . .

REITMAN: Miss Emma Goldman?

EMMA: Yes . . .

REITMAN *(grandly)*: Welcome to Chicago. An honor indeed, Miss Goldman. I am Dr. Ben Reitman. *(Bows with flourish)*
(Emma and Fedya exchange glances.)

EMMA: This is my friend Fedya.

REITMAN: A friend of Emma Goldman is a person to be cherished. *(His speech and manner are florid, grandiose.)*

FEDYA *(amused)*: Well, Emma, I leave you in good hands.
(They embrace. He goes off.)

EMMA: You are taking me to the Workers Hall?

REITMAN: No, the chief of police has closed it in anticipation of your arrival.

EMMA: Well, of course . . . *(She is sardonic.)*

REITMAN: So this morning I was asked if I would allow the use of my headquarters for your lecture.

EMMA: Your headquarters?

REITMAN: Yes, it's called Hobo Hall.

EMMA: I was told you are a doctor.

REITMAN: Indeed I am. But my work is among the city's outcasts. I have a storefront in which they stay, and my people are now setting up two hundred and fifty chairs. I assure you, they will be filled. I have spent most of the day with them putting up placards all over the city.

EMMA: *Your* people? Bums, tramps, hobos, pimps, prostitutes, petty criminals—people so destitute that both bourgeoisie

and revolutionists scorn them. You are berating me and the
anarchist movement. But how did they become *your* people?

REITMAN: I am an outcast myself. At the age of eleven, I was
on my own. I wandered the earth: work gangs in Mexico,
the San Francisco earthquake, to Europe on a tramp
steamer.

EMMA: How did you get to medical school?

REITMAN: In Chicago I found a job in a laboratory at the College of Physicians and Surgeons. One day a famous doctor
didn't show up to give his lecture. People were waiting. I
had heard him lecture before. I put on a white coat and
delivered his lecture as I remembered it.

EMMA: The school officials must have been outraged.

REITMAN: They were. But they gave me a scholarship.

EMMA: And so you became a doctor.

REITMAN: Yes, but I refuse to sell my knowledge for money. I
give it to people in need. And they give me what I need.

EMMA: Affection? Devotion? Love?

REITMAN: You understand me, and I understand you.

EMMA: Really?

REITMAN: Yes. That's why I was happy to help with your
lecture tonight.

EMMA: The police may close your place too.

REITMAN: I am on good terms with the police.

EMMA: Then you cannot be on good terms with me.

REITMAN: We have found, by diligent search, a difference
between us. I believe in speaking to everyone. Including
the police.

EMMA: Surely you know what the police do—to *your* people.

REITMAN: I know very well. Don't you think I have been
arrested? Just last week, in the march of the unemployed
here in Chicago. They knocked me around a bit in the
station house.

EMMA: And you still . . .

REITMAN: The police are no different than the prostitutes and thieves I work with every day—deprived people, acting out of desperation.

EMMA: There is truth in what you say. And also great innocence.

REITMAN: I believe I can make friends with any human being.

EMMA: You have supreme confidence in yourself.

REITMAN: I know what I can do. Just as you know what you can do. *(He takes her arm. She withdraws it.)*

EMMA: I know I can walk very well without support.

REITMAN: My object is not support.

EMMA: No?

REITMAN: No. It is to hold the arm of a woman I have admired for years.

EMMA: You don't know me.

REITMAN: I know your ideas. I know what you think about government, about prisons, about men and women.

EMMA: So you know all about me.

REITMAN: No, not all. One thing I am curious about.

EMMA: Only one thing?

REITMAN: Yes.

EMMA: What is that?

REITMAN *(quietly)*: I wonder if your breasts are as beautiful as I imagine them.

EMMA *(stepping away from him and looking directly into his face)*: Are you crazy?

REITMAN: Is it crazy to be honest?

EMMA *(laughing)*: Do you know what I am speaking about tonight?

REITMAN: No.

EMMA: About arrogant men who think they have but to touch a woman's arm to produce an orgasm of delight. And about women who are stupid enough, slavish enough, to accept that. *(Her laughter has turned to anger.)*

REITMAN: Then your speech is not about me. And not about you.

(Emma looks at him intently.)

REITMAN: Ah, here we are. *(They have been, presumably, walking towards Hobo Hall. He stops at the door.)* Can we meet after your lecture?

EMMA: I don't think so.

REITMAN: We could share some wine, talk.

EMMA: Women like me don't trust men like you.

REITMAN: There are no men like me. And no women like you.

EMMA *(deliberately)*: I don't trust *you*. *(She reaches for the door, opens it decisively, and walks through.)*

(Reitman follows, turns to face the audience, to introduce her.)

REITMAN *(bowing grandly)*: My friends, here is the woman we have all been waiting to hear, America's High Priestess of Anarchism, Miss Emma Goldman.

(Great applause. Emma comes forward to face the audience.)

EMMA: I am glad to see so many women in the audience. But tonight, my friends, I speak of the tragedy of women's emancipation. Why tragedy? Because what is now called emancipation is a delusion. There is this idea that women will be emancipated by the vote. But has the vote emancipated men? There is this idea that women will be emancipated by leaving the home and going to work. Has work emancipated men? This tragically emancipated woman is afraid to drink of the fountain of life. She is afraid of ecstasy, and so afraid of men. She will no longer be afraid of men when she learns that her freedom must come from and through herself. She must say: I am a personality, not a commodity. She must say: I refuse anyone's right over my body. I will have children or not have them as I wish. I will love and be loved as I wish. I will refuse to be a servant to God, to the State, to a husband. I will make my life simpler, deeper, richer. Such a woman will be afire with freedom, and she will light up the world for everyone!

(Applause, cheers, lights down, then up again on Emma and Reitman walking towards a table.)

REITMAN: I come here often. It's a quiet place. You should have some food. *(He holds her chair as she sits, then he does.)*

EMMA *(shaking her head)*: After a lecture, I can't eat. Some wine perhaps.

REITMAN *(calling out)*: Waiter, a bottle of bordeaux. *(Then, to Emma)* Your lecture tonight was magnificent.

EMMA: You are a good organizer. The hall was full, despite the police.

REITMAN: I know what attracts people. I am not shy about doing what is necessary for the causes I believe in. Once I stood in downtown Chicago with an open umbrella— but all that was left of the umbrella was the metal skeleton. It wasn't raining. People would stop and ask why I held this strange umbrella. I would reply: "Is it any more absurd than the system we live in, which gives you something to hold on to, a framework pretending to give protection, and results in your being drenched every time there is a downpour?"

EMMA *(laughing)*: That *is* clever.

REITMAN: More than clever. It is true. And everyone who lives in this world knows it to be true, and is just waiting for someone to say it. *(He pauses.)* Who manages your speaking tours?

EMMA: No one.

REITMAN: If I were your manager, I would double your audience. No, triple your audience.

EMMA: I know very little about you or even your ideas. I think you are Jewish. But you wear a cross. I think you are a political agitator, but you get along with the police.

REITMAN: I am a Jew by ancestry, a Baptist by choice, a socialist by conviction, a friend of policemen by practical need, and an anarchist by instinct. If I managed your lectures we would sell anarchist literature and raise money for the movement beyond anything you can imagine.

EMMA: I *was* surprised at the size of the crowd tonight.

REITMAN: I appealed to their curiosity. Many had not heard of you. I put up posters: this is Emma Goldman, the anarchist; this is Emma Goldman, the apostle of free love. And they were not disappointed tonight. Nor was I. What you said— so true. The emancipated woman, afraid of love, of passion. I know that you have no such fear.

EMMA *(amused)*: By what I said?

REITMAN: By your eyes. These extraordinary blue eyes.

EMMA: Those eyes are tired.

REITMAN: It's been a long day for you. You have a place to stay?

EMMA: I have friends in Chicago.

REITMAN: Can I count myself as one of them?

EMMA: As you like.

REITMAN: Is it a matter of indifference to you?

EMMA *(sipping her wine, smiling)*: I don't know yet.

REITMAN: How will you find out?

EMMA: Life will unfold and I will know.

REITMAN: Let us help it unfold.

EMMA: What do you mean?

REITMAN: Stay with me tonight.

EMMA: You are remarkable! We know one another for three hours.

REITMAN: You spoke tonight of passion. That has no thought of time.

EMMA: I also spoke of a women being made into a sex commodity.

REITMAN: Of course. But a woman like you? Never. No man would dare. Do you know what courage it takes to approach you? Do you know how I am trembling inside? Feel my hand.

(She looks at him directly, hesitates, takes his hand—they look at one another silently.)

REITMAN *(he speaks more softly)*: I promise you . . . a marvelous night.

EMMA *(laughing)*: Such modesty! *(She drops his hand. He touches her cheek gently and looks into her eyes.)* I am very tired, Dr. Reitman.

REITMAN: Call me Ben. But I *am* a doctor. *(He holds up his hands.)* See these hands? I want to soothe your body tonight, awaken it. It will give me great pleasure. It will give you great pleasure. It will be a rare moment in history!

EMMA: You are a little crazy! *(Pauses)* But I do like you. *(She looks at him intently, then slowly lifts her hand to stroke his hair very gently as the lights go down.)*

Scene Three

Reprise music, "Mein Ruhe Platz," signaling the old group, Vito, Anna, Fedya, sitting at a table in Vito's flat, drinking tea.

FEDYA: A good idea, Anna, to bring us together again.

ANNA: It was Emma's idea. But she's not here yet.

FEDYA *(looking around)*: You have a nice place here, Vito. How long has it been, my friends?

ANNA: Since Sasha was taken from us? Nine years.

FEDYA: Yes, a nice place, Vito. *(He lifts his head.)* But what is that smell?

VITO *(pointing to the window)*: You see down there? It's a stable.

ANNA: I love horses.

VITO: It's an elephant stable.

FEDYA: Even better.

VITO: Believe me, it lowers the rent.

FEDYA: And good for the lungs. *(He holds his nose.)*

VITO: It's true. After a day in the sewer I come home, open the window, and take a deep breath. What a pleasure! *(He goes to the window, breathes deeply, then closes the window and grasps his chest in mock pain.)*

ANNA: Vito, will you ever grow up?

FEDYA: Let us hope not. Who knows what he will grow into?

ANNA: Where is Emma? She should have been here an hour ago.

VITO: You know where she is. She's with that Reitman.

> *(The others are silent—they would rather not comment, but Vito is working himself up.)*

VITO: How can she stay with that faker?

FEDYA: It's not hard to understand. Reitman is a charmer. And he worships her. He works hard, organizes her lecture tours, goes everywhere with her. He is her serf.

VITO: And she is his slave. She seems to be—obsessed. What is there about him, Anna? Maybe you can explain.

ANNA *(smiles insinuatingly)*: I've only heard what women say. . . .

FEDYA: Women! So it's not only Emma.

ANNA: He tries with every woman he meets—short, tall, blonde, dark, young, old. He is a true democrat. He believes that all women are created equal.

FEDYA: And they talk about him?

ANNA: Women talk about men.

FEDYA: They don't talk about me. Well, maybe I haven't done

anything worth talking about. What do they say about
Reitman?

ANNA: They say he makes love like a lion. *(She growls at Fedya.)*

VITO: Does that make up for the fact that he is a liar and a
cheat?

FEDYA: Of course.

ANNA: Keep in mind that he goes everywhere with Emma,
facing the police, the mobs.

VITO: Yes, all true, but he is a circus performer, a clown, he
seeks all sensations.

ANNA: He didn't seek that incident in San Diego, where that
mob kidnapped him and tortured him, almost killed him.
He continued even after that. That shows some courage.

VITO: His courage is all in his sex organ.

FEDYA: Then his courage must be colossal.

ANNA: Oh, quiet! *(She listens.)* I hear someone on the stairs.
> *(Emma enters, embraces everyone, sits down, smoking as
> she often does. It is winter. She removes her coat.)*

EMMA: Someone out of the penitentiary today brought me a
letter from Sasha. It's not a trick. It's his writing.

VITO: Well?

EMMA: Sasha has been in and out of the basket cell—it is too
horrible to talk about. He refuses to bow down and so they
punish him, again and again. Someone else would be dead.

FEDYA: You know Sasha. He's a bull.

EMMA: In his heart, yes. But he is flesh and blood. Even with
good time, he has five years left. He has seen his friends die,
one by one. Some die of sickness. Some hang themselves in
their cells. He says he will not last five more years.
> *(Fedya, agitated, gets up, paces. Emma pauses.)*

EMMA: There is a reason he sent this letter with a friend. He
has a plan. *(She looks around.)* Anna, is the door closed?
> *(Anna checks, returns.)*

EMMA *(everyone is listening: she keeps her voice down)*: *A plan for escape*. He says there is a vacant house one hundred yards outside the prison wall. It can be rented. A tunnel can be dug from the house, under the wall, up to an abandoned wash house in the years, where he takes his walk.

VITO: A tunnel? Has Sasha gone out of his mind? I know what it takes to dig tunnels. It is impossible.

FEDYA: Poor Sasha. He has lost his senses.

ANNA: Is it so crazy?

VITO: Yes, completely crazy. It is impossible to do without being detected. It is a noisy operation. It takes more equipment than we have, more money than we have, more people than we have. More time than we have. Yes, it is completely crazy.

ANNA: What do you think, Emma?

EMMA: I think two things. First, it is, as Vito says, insane. In fact, impossible. And second . . . *(She pauses.)*

VITO *(softly)*: And second, we must do it . . . .

EMMA: Yes.

FEDYA: Yes.

ANNA: Yes, yes . . .

Scene Four

Reitman and Emma center stage, facing the audience. Ragtime music is the theme through the lecture tour.

REITMAN: Miss Goldman and I want to thank you for the hospitality you have shown us in Detroit. And now she is ready for your questions. *(He cocks his ear.)* The lady in the charming blue shawl wants to know: is it true that you believe in free love? *(He steps aside for Emma to come forward.)*

EMMA: Free love? Of course. How can it be called loose unless it is free? Is there anything more outrageous than the idea that a healthy grown woman, full of life and passion, must deny nature's demand, must subdue her most intense craving, break her spirit, stunt her vision, abstain from the depth and glory of sex until some so-called good man comes along to take her unto himself in marriage? Love, the strongest and deepest element in all life, the harbinger of hope, of joy, of ecstasy; love, the defier of all laws, of all conventions, how can such an all-compelling force by synonymous with that pitiful product of State and Church—marriage!

AUDIENCE MEMBER *(shouts)*: Miss Goldman, are you against marriage?

EMMA: I am against all institutions that demand subservience. What a world it will be when men and women cast off the church, cast off the state, refuse to sacrifice their children to the monster of war, and come together in love!

(There is a clattering of horses' hooves. Shouts. Reitman whispers in Emma's ear. She raises her hands.)

EMMA: I understand the police have surrounded the meeting hall. Please be calm. Please . . .

(Lights down.)

(Lights up again on Reitman, facing the audience. Music signals a new situation.)

REITMAN: Dear friends in Los Angeles, Miss Emma Goldman's subject tonight is "Patriotism."

EMMA *(coming forward)*: Brothers and sisters, what is patriotism? Those who have had the fortune of being born on some particular spot consider themselves better, and nobler than the living beings inhabiting any other spot. It is, therefore, the duty of everyone living on that chosen spot to fight, kill and die to impose his superiority upon all the others. Patriotism is the nourishment of war. And war is a quarrel between two thieves too cowardly to fight their own battle; therefore they take boys from one village and another village, stick them into uniforms, equip them with guns, and let them loose like wild beasts against each other. Listen to Tolstoy, who said: free yourself from the obsolete idea of patriotism and from obedience to governments. Boldly enter the region of that higher idea, the brotherly union of all people, that idea which has come to life and from all sides is calling to you. *(Applause)*

REITMAN *(coming forward)*: Are there any questions? *(He listens.)* The gentleman in back asks: does not patriotism make us a united people?

EMMA: Yes, it unites us, *against* others. It intoxicates us, and drives us to violence against anyone different from us. You need only look to the recent incident in San Diego, where a labor organizer, Joseph Mikolasek, a member of the I.W.W.—Industrial Workers of the World, how unpatriotic to be of the world!—Joseph Mikolasek was apprehended by two policemen. One had a gun, the other an axe. Together they shot and hacked Mikolasek to death. My manager and friend, Ben Reitman, dared to voice his indignation at that murder, whereupon some patriotic businessmen, pillars of the San Diego community, took him out into a deserted field, beat him, stripped him nude, threatened him with death, covered him with boiling tar, and used a red-hot branding iron to burn into his bare skin the hated letters I.W.W. Such are the results of patriotism!

AUDIENCE MEMBER *(shouts)*: The newspapers say Reitman invented that story! Dr. Reitman, you are accused of fabricating that incident. Do you want to reply?

REITMAN *(coming forward, head high, facing the audience)*: Are there reporters present? Are there photographers present? Here is my reply. . . . *(He turns, back to audience, and drops his pants—you see black scars on his backside. He quickly pulls up his pants.)* I challenge you newspapermen to place this photo alongside the face of the governor of California, and let your readers decide which picture is more attractive.

(Laughter, applause)

EMMA *(coming forward)*: Thank you for coming tonight. The meeting is adjourned.

> *(She walks off quickly as the light go down, then come up again on Emma and Ben, sitting at a table. She is drinking tea. He is eating voraciously. She is furious.)*

EMMA: Ben, you are preposterous! You embarrass me continually. You embarrass our movement. It took all my willpower to just close the meeting after your performance. Sometimes I think you will never grow up.

REITMAN *(shrugging)*: Emma, it was a joke. You and your comrades are too serious. Let's be more cheerful, less intense. It was just a joke, and to make a serious point.

EMMA: I'm not talking only about that exhibition tonight. What about last week, when that lovely old couple gave us bed and board in Detroit, and you came down to breakfast stark naked? And that meeting with the anarchist organizers in the Bronx—out of nowhere you started talking about God and Jesus. . . . And look at the outlandish way you dress. And the way you eat!

> *(He has been gobbling his food, wiping his mouth on his arm.)*

REITMAN: I eat as I do everything else, for enjoyment, not to obey the rules of etiquette. In short, my darling, I, unlike you, eat like an anarchist. *(He emphasizes this by stuffing the last bit of food into his mouth.)*

EMMA: You seem to think that anarchism has no respect for any of the ordinary niceties of behavior, like eating with some delicacy. Like bathing regularly.

REITMAN: Bathing?

EMMA: Yes, most people bathe.

REITMAN: Am I unbearable as I am? We have an hour before we catch our train. Do you really want me to spend half of it bathing? You know an hour with you is never enough, my darling. *(He wipes his mouth, stands up, pulls her to her feet, takes off her shawl gently, kisses her passionately on the throat.)*
(Emma doesn't respond at first, but he continues kissing her. She turns and throws her arms around him.)

REITMAN: You spoke wonderfully tonight, Emma. *(He continues to kiss her, to touch her.)*

EMMA: My God, Ben, I can't be angry with you.
(He keeps kissing her, buries his head in her chest.)

EMMA: My God, Ben! My God!

REITMAN: I will yet convert you to Christianity, my sweetheart. *(He kisses her again as the lights go down.)*

Scene Five

Ragtime music. Auditorium. Lights up. Emma facing audience, holds up her hand for silence.

EMMA: Brothers and sisters, the San Francisco police have said I cannot speak here tonight. There are three thousand people in this hall, and if you are here to listen to me, then, police or no police, I am here to speak to you. This past month I have gone from city to city in this nation that calls itself a democracy, speaking at sixteen meetings. Eleven were broken up by the police. We should all know by now that the Constitution of the United States does not *give* us freedom of speech—that cannot be *given*, it must be *taken*.

By people who insist on speaking, as I insist on speaking here tonight. *(Applause. She looks out into the audience.)* The young man there has a question.

YOUNG MAN *(off)*: The newspapers say you are here in San Francisco because the fleet is in the harbor and you intend to blow it up.

EMMA: No, I think I will not blow up the fleet on this visit. *(Laughter)* Bombs are not my way. But I would be happy to see the fleet sink quietly to the bottom of the sea, indeed, to see all warships everywhere in the world sink to the bottom of the sea, so that we, and our brothers and sisters in other countries, can live in peace. *(Applause)*

Scene Six

Ragtime music. Lights up on Emma and Reitman in a corner of the stage, presumably in the back of a meeting hall. Her back is to him. She is obviously wrought up.

REITMAN: I was just being pleasant to her.

EMMA: You were leading her on.

REITMAN: Not seriously. I was just playing.

EMMA *(turning around, furious)*: Don't you understand that it is wrong to play with another human being? Have you no sense of fairness or justice? Not only to me, but to these other women? I really don't know why I don't say good-bye to you once and for all. It is such hypocrisy, me speaking all over the country about women imprisoned by men, and then unable to tear myself away from you!

REITMAN: Don't berate yourself. It's my fault. My weakness. It was just one night.

EMMA *(enraged)*: So you did spend the night! You liar! You said: "I can't be in Chicago and not see my mother." You spent the night with that woman.

> *(She is beside herself, starts punching Reitman. He grabs her arms.)*

EMMA: You liar!

REITMAN: Please, Emma, stop that. I have to introduce you in two minutes. Calm down. We'll talk afterward, my darling.

EMMA: We'll *fuck* afterward, my darling! No, not this time! Get out there and do your introduction. And don't wait for me at the hotel afterward. The committee will find me a place to stay.

> *(Reitman shakes his head ruefully, goes to face the audience, wiping his forehead with his kerchief.)*

REITMAN *(moving center stage to address the audience)*: Dear friends in New Kensington. What a pleasure to be in the beautiful state of Pennsylvania. I give you Miss Emma Goldman, speaking on "The Drama of Henrik Ibsen."

> *(Applause.)*

EMMA: My brothers and sisters. *(She glances at Reitman angrily, then composes herself.)* We all know that in the home not everything can be said. We know that in the factory or wherever one works for a boss, not everything can be said. But on the stage, one can speak freely. And so the drama can be used to conquer ignorance, fear, prejudice. There is ignorance and prejudice about the most fundamental things of life. I am speaking of love and marriage. What does love have to do with marriage? The answer is: nothing. The wife, like the prostitute, is a commodity to be bought, the prostitute for a night, the wife for much longer.

AUDIENCE MEMBERS *(shouting)*: "You are the whore!" "Who invited you?" "Get her off the stage!"

EMMA: Yes, the truth is hard to listen to. The man I have made so angry there in the first row is probably a husband who doesn't want his wife to hear her own secret thoughts spoken aloud.

AUDIENCE MEMBER *(shouts)*: I'm getting out of here!

EMMA: I'm sorry to see you go, sir. I wish you could hear about Henrik Ibsen. Ibsen's great play, *A Doll's House*, is about a woman, Nora. She has been living for eight years with a stranger. In a lovely house. A doll's house. But she has come to a decision. She is not a doll. She is a woman. And who is this stranger she has been living with? Her husband. Is it degrading for a prostitute to sleep for a night with a stranger? Then how degrading is an intimacy between two strangers, man and wife, which lasts a lifetime? Let us be careful, then, before we denounce prostitutes, before we brand them with that scarlet letter, because they are very much like women, for whom we should have compassion as they struggle for their souls, their bodies, their freedom.

(Applause. Lights dim)

Scene Seven

Lights up on Emma and Almeda Sperry sitting at a kitchen table. She is a good-looking woman in her mid-thirties, dressed somewhat flamboyantly, wearing make-up.

ALMEDA: All right, I'll call you Emma. And you call me Almeda. Sperry's my last name, but no one round here knows it. It was so goddamn thrilling tonight to hear you talk about Ibsen. I have read *A Doll's House* three times. But I never could find anyone to talk with about it.

EMMA: I noticed you in the audience. I thought, that pretty woman, sitting there so rapt, looks like an actress.

ALMEDA: No, not me. But I love everything on stage. I almost committed suicide because Sarah Bernhardt was coming here and I was broke. But a guy gave me a dollar. I won't tell you what I gave him. But it was worth it. I sat up in goose haven and cried every time she spoke her lines.

EMMA: You live here alone?

ALMEDA: I have a husband—that's Fred. He calls himself my husband, but I don't think he is. He's not around much, no one worth talking about. How about you?

EMMA: I have a sweetheart. No one worth talking about.

(They laugh.)

ALMEDA: That fella who introduced you? A handsome devil.

EMMA: Devil. That's the right word.

ALMEDA: Yeah, I know men like that. I could tell you stories all night.

EMMA: I'd like to hear them. I could learn a few things.

ALMEDA: And you tell me about Shaw and Strindberg. Never could find anything they wrote. Hey, I'll make some hot tea. Got biscuits too. I'd offer some booze, but I drank it all before the meeting. That's my weakness. Well, not the only one. I know about handsome devils. Believe me, Emma, there's hardly anything anyone can tell me about men. I don't dare tell you how many men I have been with. And I'm still waiting to meet a *man*. Not just a biped who thinks he's a man because he has this thing.

EMMA: I do know a real man. He's in prison.

ALMEDA: I heard about him. It happened right here in Pennsylvania. Pittsburgh. Frick. The strike. I heard. Do you visit him?

EMMA *(shaking her head)*: They won't let me near him.

ALMEDA: How long has it been?

EMMA: Nine years.

(They are silent, sip their tea.)

ALMEDA: Does he know about your sweetheart?

EMMA: Yes and no.

ALMEDA: I know what you mean. Jealousy is strange. Fred is jealous of my friend Florence, who is Irish, French, and Jewish. She has beautiful, dark hair and soft hands. She thinks that a woman should have each kid by a different man. That's what she thinks of marriage. What you said about marriage and prostitution, I couldn't believe you were saying it out loud. I have thought that for years. Men have used me, Emma. And I have used men. Just because I was short of money. You were saying the truth.

EMMA: I'm not saying something new. Just things people have been afraid to say in public.

ALMEDA: You do say it. I wish I could talk like that. I think I could though if not for drinking too much. But I need it with this lousy life, not just my life, but all around, people climbing up that steep hill so tired, slipping back, but climbing. You know why I married Fred? Hey! Your eyes are closing. God, I didn't think how tired you must be coming in all night on the Pennsylvania Railroad, then talking your guts out. And tomorrow, I heard you say you got to be in New York for the big demonstration—the Depression has hit New York bad, just like here. And I am going on like this. . . . You go to bed, Emma. . . .

EMMA *(waking up)*: No, I'm listening. Please . . .

ALMEDA: You sure? I was saying how I got to marry Fred. It was to get out of my mother's house because it was so cold. She would never turn up the gas for fear of a big bill. And I was sick, coughing, and Fred took me out of there, and so I'm grateful to him, though he has lacerated my soul.

(Emma is falling off again. Almeda walks over behind her and gently massages her back and neck. Emma opens her eyes and clasps Almeda's hand as the lights go down.)

Scene Eight

Union Square. Emma appears center stage, revolutionary music in the background. She gets up on a box, to address an enormous crowd of the unemployed. Her style here is different than the lecture platform. This is a rally.

EMMA: Look around, my friends, look around! Thousands of working men and working women have come here today to Union Square to declare their anger at this system, which has no jobs for people willing to work. All over the city, the lines of the unemployed stretch for miles. In the richest city in the world! Yes, the richest city in the world, and women must sell their bodies just to stay alive! The richest city in the world, and children are crying for food.

(A group of shabbily dressed men and women gather around her, as if her talk is a magnet, drawing them in; they are humming "Mein Greene Kuzine.")

EMMA: We ask for work and they tell us to wait. We ask for medicine for the sick, and they tell us to pray. We ask for food and they tell us to vote.

(Police appear suddenly.)

EMMA: We ask for time to pay the rent, and they send the police. Yes, the police are here as always, to protect the rich. Brothers and sisters *(her tone rises)* . . . if the children need milk, let us go into the stores and take it. If families need bread, let us find out where the flour is stored and take it.

(The police move toward her.)

EMMA: Take it! Take it!

(Police grab her roughly and pull her off the platform as the lights go down and the hoofbeats of the police forces get louder.)

Scene Nine

Two men in a darkened office, the better to view photos, which are illumined by a spotlight. One man is slim, well-dressed, striped suit, lawyer-like. This is Attorney General Thomas Gregory. The other, a young man, stocky, hair slicked back, is J. Edgar Hoover, who is showing the photos—but he won't be identified until the very end of the scene. As they go through the photos, perhaps a projection of each appears on a screen for the audience.

HOOVER *(showing a photo)*: This was last September.

GREGORY: What was she charged with?

HOOVER: Trespassing. She had brought women into the Smokers' Club in Minneapolis. A men's club.

GREGORY: A brazen one, isn't she? What is that sign she is carrying outside the club?

HOOVER: It says: "I am a heavy smoker."

GREGORY: I understand she travels everywhere with a man younger than herself.

HOOVER: Yes, his name is Reitman. He manages lectures. Our informants tell us that they have engaged in numerous immoral sexual acts. Never overt enough to make an arrest.

GREGORY *(taking another photo in his hands)*: What is this one?

HOOVER: New York City, the lower East Side. It was a meeting of Jewish women. She told them how to use contraceptives.

GREGORY: How much time did she get for that?

HOOVER: She was released for lack of evidence. It seems she spoke to the group entirely in the Jewish language, and our informant could not understand a word.

GREGORY: Is this the lot?

HOOVER: No sir. This is a partial record. She has been arrested fourteen times.

GREGORY: Where is she now?

HOOVER: She is serving a one-year sentence on Blackwell's Island. Inciting a riot.

GREGORY: But she'll be out soon and back to her old tricks. Just as the situation in Cuba is getting serious.

HOOVER: We are looking for a way to deport her. Back to Russia.

GREGORY: That would be ideal. But I understand she was married once to an American citizen.

HOOVER: Yes, when she was seventeen. To one Jacob Kershner, a naturalized citizen, and so she automatically became a citizen under the law.

GREGORY: Well, our laws were not intended to make the country helpless before its enemies.

HOOVER: We are working on the problem, sir.

GREGORY: I'm glad to hear that.

HOOVER: It is a challenge. We are dealing with the most dangerous woman in America.

GREGORY: Thank you, Mr. Hoover.

Scene Ten

Prison. Emma, center stage, sitting on her prison cot, writing.
In three different parts of the stage, by turns in darkness or lighted,
sit Sasha, in prison uniform; Reitman in characteristic garb; and
Almeda Sperry. They all speak from their own letters.

SASHA: My dearest Emma. I heard that your speech in Union
Square was magnificent, and that you have been sentenced
to a year in Blackwell's Island. Please take care of yourself.
The guards found an escape tunnel—they didn't know who
was responsible but they decided to punish me anyway—
the stomach pump every morning, the straitjacket every
night. For seven days and nights. I lost consciousness, I
don't know for how long. But I woke up this morning and
heard a sparrow singing outside my window, and thought:
I must be alive.

EMMA: My darling Ben. I am ashamed and horrified because
of what has become of me since I met you. Sasha risked his
life, surrendered his freedom, for all of us. I wrote him that
I couldn't sleep all night thinking of him. That was a lie.
Most of the night I lie awake thinking of you. Thinking of
that first night in Chicago when you aroused me as no man
has ever aroused me, when you took me like a hurricane
and I forgot everything and everybody.

REITMAN: You know I love Sasha as you do. Don't torment
yourself. Life is what it is. Love is what it is. How I wish
I can be with you, to massage your tired body, to kiss every
inch of it.

EMMA: Last night I lay on my cot, trembling, my throat choked,
as it always is when we come together, in that moment
before your first embrace.

REITMAN: I want to be with you. Gloom has my soul. I am
   afraid you will forget.

EMMA: Darling Ben. Why do I think so much of you? I should
   be thinking of the work that must be done when I get
   out of here. The country is going mad with war fever over
   Cuba. I do think of these things. But very soon your image
   appears and crowds out everything else. How I want you!
   I want to devour you.

REITMAN: You are my whole world. How terrible it is to love.

EMMA: I sometimes get angry. I think of your infidelities, your
   rotten infidelities, your lies, your excuses. And then I lie
   back, my eyes closed, and I forget everything for want of
   you . . .

ALMEDA: Dearest Emma. Fred is angry with me tonight
   because I gave a bucket of soup and a loaf of homemade
   bread to my friend Irene. She runs a stock company here
   in the summer and plays in little jerkwater towns in the
   winter. How are you, my dear moonbeam, shimmering on
   a dark pool at night, my drop of dew hidden in the heart
   of a wild rose?

EMMA: Accept my love for what it is, and for what it cannot be.
   But it is there, and real.

ALMEDA: How sweet of you to say the things you said to me
   in your last letter. Yes, I remember that wonderful day-
   evening-night-morning we had together in-between your
   Pittsburgh speech and your Philadelphia rally. It made me
   stop drinking. Then my mother died. We never did get
   along, but when she was near gone I went to see her.
   I kissed her hand and she began to cry. When she left
   this earth, it rained all day, and I drank and drank.

EMMA: Don't ask, as you once did, am I, Almeda, really a socialist or anarchist or what am I? It doesn't matter. Just do what

your instincts tell you, be what you are so naturally, so honest, so direct, so impossible to give a name to.

ALMEDA: Dear Emma. I'll never forget the day you took me in your arms and I kissed your beautiful throat, the throat of a bird I once saw. Your eyes are like violets in the morning. I know your work comes first, the cause comes first, but when your time is up I will come to see you wherever you are. Some days I want a baby so bad, don't you? You told me once you did, you told me how you thought you were having one and then it was a mistake. That was the first time I ever saw you cry.

REITMAN: Dearest Emma. I'm going to Pennsylvania tomorrow to sell some good literature and organize a fund for political prisoners. I will look up your friend in New Kensington. I think she is on the sponsoring committee for my talk. . . .

ALMEDA: Dear Emma. Your boyfriend Reitman came to New Kensington. He is a strange bird. Some day I'll tell you about it.

> *(Sound of steel doors clanging. Voice, off: "Goldman! Goldman!" Lights down. Then up again, as clanging of steel doors continues, then stops. A woman—she could be a black or white woman in her forties, definitely Southern— is sitting and sewing her nurse's smock. A matron brings in Emma, who can barely walk, and who sits down immediately on a cot.)*

MATRON: Lizbeth, here's a new helper for you. She's just outta solitary. The warden says to teach her good, keep her out of trouble. *(She leaves.)*

LIZBETH *(goes over to Emma, who is hunched over)*: Now don't sit squinched up like that. You not in solitary any more. You better start using your legs, else you'll never be able to walk again. Now get up. *(She pulls her up and helps her walk in a tiny circle while continuing to talk.)* What they got you in solitary for? *(Looks into Emma's face)* No need to tell me. You're that Red Emma they talk about. They say you don't take sass from no one. They say you put in charge of the sewing room and they wanted you get the girls working faster and you wouldn't, no-how. *(She laughs.)* Yeah, I hear them talk about you. They say you want to change the whole world. . . . I hear somethin' else. I hear you got a handsome boyfriend brings you home-baked cookies, and you give them out to everybody. Now see here, Emma, I just love home-baked cookies! *(She laughs. Emma smiles weakly. She is beginning to come alive.)* You know me? *(Emma shakes her head.)* I'm Lizbeth. I'm the prison nurse. They wants you to help me in the hospital ward. And I'm goin' to teach you all kinds of things. Startin' right now. Lay yourself down. Like this. *(Gently pushes her down. She massages Emma's legs.)* You got to know when to make people walk, and when to make them keep still. You got to know when to rub hard, and when to rub gentle. You got to know when to use a cold compress, and when to use a hot one. Hey, why do they call you Red Emma?

EMMA: It's a long story.

LIZBETH: We got lots o' time in here. *(She laughs at this ancient prison joke.)* You tell me about that, and I'll tell you what to do when a woman starts bleeding down there. . . . You ever bring a baby into the world?

(Emma shakes her head.)

LIZBETH: Emma, you bring someone's baby into the world, and you can do just about anything. Next week there's a girl up in the ward about to have her birth. And you are goin' to help me. *(She takes Emma's wrist and puts her fingers on her pulse.)* Now first thing, I'm goin' to teach you to take a pulse. You put your fingers here. *(She holds out her wrist.)* Feel that? That's my life, beatin' for you. Won't stop no

matter what. Goes on beatin', on and on. Isn't that beautiful? *(She looks into Emma's face.)* You want to learn nursing,
Emma?

EMMA: I want you to teach me, Lizbeth.

LIZBETH: I will teach you. Now I want you to remember one
thing.

EMMA: What?

LIZBETH: I just *love* home-baked cookies! *(She laughs
uproariously.)*

   (Emma manages a smile, as the scene ends.)

Scene Eleven

*Thalia Theater. Music from Verdi. Shouts: "Welcome home Emma!"
Singing. She comes on stage, to address her friends, there to greet her
return from prison. She is low-key, a little pale.*

EMMA: It's strange. Do you know, I tried two years ago to
investigate prison conditions. They wouldn't let me near a
prison. Then, suddenly, a stroke of luck. *(She smiles.)* I was
inside! *(Shakes her head)* Oh, I learned so much in this year
on Blackwell's Island. And what I learned I'll never forget.
(She pauses.) Being there made me think, even more than
before, about our comrade, Alexander Berkman. *(Applause)*
And all the others who fill the prisons. *(She chokes up a little,
remembering.)* And I promised myself, day after day inside
that hell, listening to the other women, marveling as I took
their pulses that their hearts could beat so strongly in defiance of their condition. . . . I promised myself that I would
not rest until the prisons of this country are taken apart,
brick by brick, and the iron bars melted down, to make

playgrounds for our children. . . . It's good to be back with you, my brothers and sisters. . . .

(Music rises, fades.)

Scene Twelve

A darkened room, in a tenement. Music recalls family gathering from Scene 1. Emma comes in with a lighted candle.

EMMA: Helena, my darling sister, where are you? Don't you have any light?

HELENA: Here—I'm in bed. I ran out of kerosene last week. I'm so glad you're here. I haven't seen you since papa passed away. And I had to bring you that news.

EMMA: It was strange. I had so often cursed him, wished he were dead. But then when it happened I thought, he was just a working man, his life was hard, and his cruelty was the cruelty of his own life.

HELENA: It was right after that you went to Europe.

EMMA: To Vienna. To learn to be a midwife.

HELENA: I was so excited to hear that. I thought, I want Emma to bring out my baby, no one else. Am I your first?

EMMA *(shakes her head)*: In Vienna, I delivered six babies. No, seven. One woman had twins. And just last week on the East Side. The woman was so sick; it was a foul and miserable room. But she gave birth to a beautiful black-haired baby. You should have seen it, Helena. It came out with clenched fists, what a fighter!

HELENA: A boy?

EMMA: A girl.

(They both laugh.)

EMMA: How far along are you?

HELENA: Maybe seven months. You can see . . .

EMMA: Yes. *(She peers at her.)* You have good color in your face. *(She takes her wrist.)* Your pulse is regular. *(She touches her.)* Does this hurt?

HELENA: No, it feels good.

EMMA: Now let me listen. *(She places her stethoscope against Helena's belly.)*

HELENA: What are you listening for?

EMMA: Ssshh!

HELENA: You're listening for the heartbeat. You hear it?

EMMA: Don't talk now. *(She listens.)*

HELENA: Do you hear it? You should hear it!

EMMA: We'll try again in a few minutes. Sometimes it takes a while. Now just relax. Tell me about Mama.

HELENA: Mama's all right. She sits all day and sews. How's Sasha? Did they ever let you see him?

EMMA *(shakes her head, then turns her face away to control herself)*: Sasha was sure he would not come out alive. We were desperate. Our comrades began to dig a tunnel. It's hard to believe. Such a crazy idea. But they did it. They were inches away from the prison yard, and it was discovered. A really crazy idea. But it almost worked. They weren't sure it was for Sasha, but they punished him anyway. *(She closes her eyes, then shakes off the memory.)*

HELENA: Is it true there's another man you are with?

EMMA: Yes. A sensitive, beautiful man—on Mondays, Wednesdays, Fridays. On Tuesdays, Thursdays, Saturdays, Sundays—an insensitive monster. *(Sighs)* Helena, have you ever been so infatuated, so physically infatuated with a man that it made you insane?

HELENA: Just the opposite. For me it was the absence of such a feeling that made me insane. You know my marriage . . .

EMMA: Yes.

HELENA: But I do want this child. So much. Emma, try again.

EMMA *(applying the stethoscope again, listening)*: Sometimes . . .

HELENA: I'm nervous, Emma! You know I've lost two. I want this baby so much. You understand. You love children. I hope to have a child some day, Emma.

EMMA: You know my condition.

HELENA: But the doctors said: an operation . . .

EMMA: Doctors! One had me believing last year I was pregnant. For two months I believed it. How happy I was! Then the same doctor, very calm, said: "Oh, a mistake!" I wanted to kill her. I cried for a week. No one knew. I just disappeared for a whole week and cried.

HELENA: You'll have the operation, then.

EMMA: No. A woman has the right to decide not to have children, doesn't she?

HELENA: Of course. But . . .

EMMA: Now I'm a midwife. I can bring all kinds of children into the world. That makes me happy. *(She places the stethoscope again.)* Sshh! *(She hands the earpiece to Helena, who listens.)*

HELENA: I hear something. . . .

EMMA: That's your baby. A strong, strong beat.

HELENA *(throwing her arms around Emma)*: Oh my God!

EMMA: Come, let's walk. It's good for you and your baby. *(They start to walk around the room.)* You know, Helena, I'm going to bring a million little babies into the world. And as they come out of their mothers' wombs, I will whisper in their tiny ears: "Rebel! Rebel! Join together! Change the world!" And in one generation . . .

HELENA: Emma! Don't you get arrested before my time comes!

Scene Thirteen

Buffalo, New York. An outdoor gathering. Military music.

ANNOUNCER *(off)*: Fellow citizens, the president of the United
    States!
    *(Band strikes up. President William McKinley mounts the
    platform.)*
MCKINLEY: My fellow Americans . . . I am indeed happy to
    be present at this splendid Exposition in the historic city
    of . . . *(Pauses to remember)* Buffalo. It is a pleasure to report
    to you that our great nation is in good health. Business
    is prospering. Overseas, our war with Spain has yielded
    the most happy results. War is always to be regretted.
    But . . . Cuba is now free and under our protection. Puerto
    Rico is ours. Hawaii fell like a ripe fruit into our arms. I did
    puzzle for some time on what to do with the Philippines,
    and then I got down on my knees and prayed to God, and
    He said: "Take them, Mr. President. Civilize them, Chris-
    tianize them. . . ." And so . . .
    (A shot is heard. Silence)
    *(Lights up on reporters milling about, notebooks in hand.
    Reitman appears, in his usual get-up.)*
REITMAN: Gentlemen, she will be here in a moment.
    *(Emma walks on stage, immediately surrounded by the
    reporters.)*
REPORTER: Miss Goldman, after President McKinley was shot,
    why did they arrest *you?*
EMMA: You are reporters. You know the police don't need
    evidence to arrest someone. The president was assassinated.
    A government always goes into a frenzy when someone else

uses its own tactic. *(Her mood is calm, good-humored in all this.)*

REPORTER: Its own tactic?

EMMA: Murder.

REPORTER: Radical organizations all over the country have repudiated the assassin Czolgosz. It is said that you defend him.

EMMA: I defend him, not his act, but his anguish.

REPORTER: Do you believe Czolgosz is insane?

EMMA: He must be. He killed one man, with no force of law behind him. If he were the president of the United States he could do as McKinley did, send an army into the Philippines to kill ten-year-old children. That would be legal. And perfectly sane.

REPORTER: Is it true you offered to nurse the president after he was wounded?

EMMA: Yes. *(A hint of a smile)* But for some reason, my offer was not accepted.

REPORTER: Then you feel compassion for the president?

EMMA: Of course. You must feel compassion for a president who doesn't know where the Philippines are until the merchants and bankers point it out to him on the map.

REPORTER: You are quoted as saying that the business interests benefitted from the war.

EMMA: I know one thing. The working classes got nothing from it. They never do. Their sons died in those islands. And when the smoke of battle was gone, and the dead buried, the cost of the war came home to the families of the dead, in higher prices for food and rent.

REPORTER: Your friend Berkman is in prison for an attempted assassination. Does he approve of what Czolgosz did?

EMMA: When he is released from prison you can ask him yourself. But I can tell you that neither Berkman nor I believe, as some of us once did, that assassination is a step towards revolution.

REPORTER: Have you decided then that the way to change is through the ballot box?

EMMA: The ballot box? Voting is a game, to keep everyone busy while the rich take control of the nation's wealth. When Rockefeller wants an oil refinery does he take a vote? When McKinley wants the Philippines, does he take a vote?

REPORTER: Then what do you propose?

EMMA: People will organize, wherever they work, wherever they live. And when they are strong enough, they will take back this country, take back everything that was stolen from them. It's much simpler than voting.

REPORTER: Can we quote you on all this?

EMMA *(smiling)*: Will your newspapers print all this?

> *(Music louder, Reitman takes her by the arm as the lights go down.)*

Scene Fourteen

Railroad station. Spring. Dusk. Railroad whistle. Sound of engine starting up, train moving away. A man is standing, back to audience, stage right, wearing a hat, an oversized coat, carrying a small suitcase. He is motionless. Emma comes in stage left, stops. She is carrying flowers. She sees the man, studies him a moment, then calls hesitantly.

EMMA: Sasha?

> *(The man doesn't move at first. Then he turns and looks at her, remains where he is. She takes some steps toward him, stops. He doesn't answer. She moves to him. He nods his*

*head. She throws her arms around him and they embrace,
in silence, then break away. She holds out the flowers. He
takes them, closes his eyes, presses his lips against the flowers.
Lights down)*

Scene Fifteen

*Lights up on Sachs's Café. A reprise of the Sachs's Café music. Vito
and Anna arrive, sit down at a table. They are better dressed than
in the old days. They are fourteen years older.*

VITO *(calling out)*: Mr. Sachs! *(Turns to Anna)* It's still the same
service.
    (Mr. Sachs arrives.)
SACHS: Vito! Anna! After all these years! *(He grasps their
hands.)* Vito, you're still complaining. But it's good to see
you back. Tell me, do you still work in the sewers?
VITO: Do I look like a man who works in the sewers?
SACHS *(looks him over carefully)*: You look more prosperous.
You look like a man who once worked in the sewers.
VITO: You are a perceptive man, Mr. Sachs. I have risen in the
world. I am a bookkeeper for the Sewer Department.
SACHS: Hmmm. Who would believe that the Sewer Department keeps books? And you, Anna?
ANNA: I'm not in the factory any more. I'm an organizer for
the garment union.
SACHS: Still *tumuling*. I knew it. Tell me, have I changed?
VITO: A little more gray in your hair. A little more distin-
guished-looking. But your table cloths are the same. Don't
you think, after fourteen years you should change table
cloths?

SACHS *(sighs)*: The same Vito. A wonderful person. Just a little crazy. How about a little wine to sober you up? I know it's a special day. Where are the others?

ANNA: Here comes the wine!

> *(Fedya has arrived, carrying a bottle. He is dressed elegantly. She and Vito get up and embrace Fedya. Sachs, standing off, observes Fedya.)*

SACHS: Beautiful! Beautiful!

FEDYA: Good to see you, Mr. Sachs. *(Shakes his hand)* How about some glasses? You'll drink with us.

SACHS: Like old times. You bring your own wine. I supply the glasses. It's a miracle I'm still in business.

ANNA *(excitedly)*: They're here!

> *(Emma and Sasha have arrived. Anna gets up, goes to Sasha. They embrace.)*

SASHA: Anna! Dear Anna!

> *(He is not the old, strong-looking, confident Sasha. He is a little bent, more subdued in manner. He turns and embraces Vito, then looks and sees Fedya. Fedya brushes a tear from his eye, comes over and embraces Sasha, then Emma. Vito pulls chairs over for them. They sit down. Sachs comes in with a tray of glasses.)*

SACHS *(putting down the tray, grasps Sasha's hand)*: Sasha! Sasha! So good to see you. So many years. What you have been through! Have something to eat. It's my treat.

SASHA *(shakes his head, speaks quietly)*: I'm not hungry, Mr. Sachs. I'll just sit a while.

SACHS: This is something new, Sasha refusing food! I never . . .

EMMA: Enough, Mr. Sachs.

SACHS: What did I say? Did I say something wrong?

VITO: It's all right, Mr. Sachs. Nothing wrong. *(Turns to Sasha)* Sasha, you should have some food.

EMMA: Don't tell him what to do, Vito. *(They are all on edge.)*

VITO: Don't do this, don't do that! Forgive me, Emma.

SACHS: Look. *(Holds out a newspaper)* Look, in the afternoon paper, a picture of you, Sasha, an old one. *(He reads.)* "Alexander Berkman, Frick assailant, released after fourteen years."

>*(Vito takes the paper, reads, looks up.)*

VITO: There's something about you, too, Emma, on the opposite page. He hands it to her.

>*(She reads.)*

FEDYA: What is it?

EMMA: The government has revoked the citizenship of Jacob Kershner, my former husband. That means I am no longer a citizen. And so . . . *(She is pensive.)* The hypocrites. How they play with the law.

ANNA: Will they try to deport you now, Emma?

EMMA: Perhaps. Or they will wait, until I break some federal law.

FEDYA: It's too depressing. Let's drink a toast. To Sasha's return.

>*(They all drink.)*

SASHA *(softly)*: Thank you, dear friends. I . . . *(He is interrupted by sounds from the street, marching music, singing.)*

>*(Sachs goes to the door.)*

FEDYA: What is it, Mr. Sachs?

SACHS *(still looking out into the street)*: I don't know. I see soldiers and sailors marching. *(He calls out into the street.)* What's the parade? *(Someone in the street responds. Sachs returns to the group. He is very solemn.)* President Wilson has asked Congress to declare war on Germany.

>*(Everyone is silent.)*

FEDYA: First Europe goes mad. Now America.

ANNA: Congress will be voting very quickly. They become like sheep when a president asks for war. We have to move fast.

VITO: This was expected, Anna. A rally has already been called

for next week. At the Harlem River Casino. Emma is one
of the speakers.

ANNA: Emma must not speak. Now with this news about
Kershner and her citizenship, they will pounce on her in a
minute.

EMMA: I cannot be silent now. If I cannot speak at a moment
like this, everything I have done up to now is worthless.

FEDYA: Emma, it would be a mistake.

(They are all silent.)

SASHA *(speaking up for the first time, causing everyone to turn his
way—he speaks softly)*: Emma, I think Fedya is right. You
can miss one meeting. I will speak in your place.

ANNA *(alarmed)*: No, Sasha! Fourteen years is enough.

SASHA: They have silenced me all these years. It is time for me
to speak. I must.

EMMA *(putting her arms around Sasha)*: Let it be both of us.
Sasha and I. We will both speak against the war.

(Everyone is silent.)

SACHS: My dear friends. *(Wipes a tear from his eye)* Let's open a
bottle of wine. Sasha is back with us!

(Lights down)

Scene Sixteen

*Music. Reitman and Emma in a room. He has just come in. She is
clearly upset by his presence, keeps her distance.*

EMMA: Why did you come, Ben? You stayed away six months.
And here you are, just before I am to speak. They are
expecting six thousand people.

REITMAN: My darling! When I heard the news, that war was
   declared, I knew I must come to you. I am frightened for
   you, Emma. Today Wilson signs the Conscription Law, and
   tonight, anyone who speaks against it . . . You know what
   they want to do to you. Don't speak tonight.

EMMA: I don't need your advice.

REITMAN: Why so cold, my sweetheart? Why so utterly cold?
   What is going on? Is it because I can't join you in this? It's
   not my way. I don't believe in putting our heads into their
   nooses.

EMMA: Someone must. If we can only persist, we will be too
   many for their nooses.

REITMAN: Dreams, dreams, Emma. How I love your dreams.
   But I am afraid for you with your dreams. I can't stand the
   thought of you in prison again. And what if they send you
   out of the country? What would I do without you? You, my
   sweetheart, my Venus, my love!

EMMA: Enough, Ben. Your one concern is: what will *you* do?

REITMAN: Have I not stood with you? Have I not faced down
   howling mobs, from here to California?

EMMA: Yes. I never understood why. You were never one of
   us. . . .

REITMAN: My God, so cold, Emma, so cold. What is wrong?
   Why can't we just be happy? You and your friends—they
   cannot stand joy. They cannot be at peace. Wilson declares
   war. You declare war. Why is that necessary? Let Wilson
   sign his act. Let those who don't want to fight not fight.
   Why must we stand on platform and exhort and push and
   trumpet our defiance? They are setting a trap for us, Emma.
   Be careful tonight, Emma. And think of Sasha. Can he
   survive another term in prison?

EMMA: You're not thinking of Sasha. You're thinking of yourself.

REITMAN: My darling, you're upset for some reason.

> *(He reaches for her, she turns away, pulls a letter from her pocket.)*

EMMA: I received a letter from Almeda Sperry.

REITMAN: Almeda Sperry . . . I'm trying to remember. . . .

EMMA: What a bad memory my poor Ben has! Almeda Sperry. She met you when you went to speak in Pennsylvania.

REITMAN *(suddenly remembering)*: Oh yes, that drunken socialist whore in New Kensington.

EMMA *(angry)*: "That drunken socialist whore"?! Who sold herself to men when she had nothing to eat? Who single-handedly built a socialist group in that godforsaken little town? The most straight-speaking person I have ever known? Listen. *(She reads from the letter.)* "Darling Emma, I am amused by Reitman. But don't ever send him to New Kensington again. I have had a deep horror of him ever since he met me at the railroad station. I understood him thoroughly as soon as he took my arm the way he did when we walked along the street. Please ask him, for the sake of the Cause, if he ever goes to meet another sinful woman who is beginning to see a glimmer of light—please ask him, for humanities sake, for his own sake and the woman's sake—not to begin *fuck talk*."

REITMAN: She writes vividly. . . . Truth is, I'm not sure what she's talking about.

EMMA: You are such a liar.

REITMAN: Have I ever denied it? I would be lying if I did, and why add one more to my long history? But how can one live in this world without lying, Emma?

EMMA: Lying to your enemies, perhaps. To those you love, that is unpardonable.

REITMAN: But that is what is wonderful about you, Emma. You have always pardoned the unpardonable.

EMMA: Yes, Ben. I have always pardoned everything in you.

> *(She turns from him. He puts his arms around her, kisses her neck.)*

EMMA: Oh, that first time you took me by the arm. How you took me by the arm! How angry I was! How thrilled I was! *(She turns and embraces him.)*

REITMAN *(gently)*: I was not playing with you, Emma. I have stayed with you, year after year.

> *(She breaks away.)*

EMMA: Yes, you have. On and off. Steadfast and deceitful. You always made me forget everything else when I was with you. I was ashamed of my craving for you and yet I couldn't stop. What a sham! I speak all over America about the independence of women and then I rush to you. You have made life so worth living, you bastard! *(She presses against him, grasps his hair as if to hurt him. He winces. She breaks away.)* I have to go to speak. This is ridiculous!

REITMAN: Will we meet after you speak?

EMMA: No. Not tonight. Not any night. Not any more.

REITMAN: I will miss you, my blue-eyed darling.

EMMA: Will you be at the meeting?

REITMAN: I have a train ticket to Chicago. But I can wait until tomorrow if only you and I . . .

> *(She shakes her head, starts to leave.)*

REITMAN: Please, Emma, be careful tonight. Criticize Wilson. Condemn the war. But there will be draft-age young men in the audience. If you urge them to refuse conscription, the government is ready to spring. We need you and Sasha.

EMMA: Good-bye, dear Ben.

> *(She starts to leave, turns back, for a long, passionate kiss, then breaks off quickly and walks off without looking back. Reitman looks after her, then straightens his tie, picks up his cane, and walks off in the other direction.)*

Scene Seventeen

Harlem River Casino. Huge crowd. Taped crowd noises. Music.
Emma and Sasha sitting on chairs, facing the audience.

SASHA: You said you wouldn't see Ben Reitman again.

EMMA: He came to me.

> *(Sounds of crashing glass.)*

SASHA: The sailors in the balcony. Look, they're unscrewing the
light bulbs and . . .

> *(Crash of lightbulbs around them.)*

EMMA: Ben and I are finished.

SASHA: But are you finished with . . . with what you wanted in
him?

> *(More crashing of glass lightbulbs around them.)*

EMMA *(turns to look at Sasha)*: Never, Sasha. Never finished with
that.

SASHA: You're being introduced.

> *(They listen. Emma rises and faces the audience.)*

EMMA *(waits for crashing light bulbs to stop before she addresses the
audience in a loud clear voice)*: So this is the war to make the
world safe for democracy! Thank you, friends in the balcony, for clarifying that. *(Silence, then another crash, laughter.
Emma points up to the balcony.)* You, young man, put that
down, and tell us what is on your mind.

AUDIENCE MEMBER IN BALCONY: I was born in this country,
and I'm willing to die for this country!

> *(Yells of approval around him)*

EMMA *(waits for noise to die down)*: I, too, am willing to die for
this country. *(Silence. Her voice rises.)* Yes, for this *country*.
For the mountains and rivers, the land, the *people*, yes, for
the *country*. But not for the president, not for the gener-

als and admirals, not for the industrialists and bankers who want this war. *They* are not our country. They do not care a damn whether you, young man, live or die. What is patriotism, my friends? Is it love of your government? No, it is love of your country, of your fellow men and women. And that love, *that* patriotism, may require you to oppose the government. *(Applause)* Mark this day, my friends. The eighteenth of May 1917. The president has signed the Conscription Law, and the young men of this nation will now be marched into the slaughterhouse of the war in Europe. I say to you, young men in the balcony, and young men everywhere. Refuse to die! Refuse to kill! If you have a mind of your own, a will of your own, if you do not want to be a slave of authority, if you believe in democracy and liberty and peace for all mankind, refuse, refuse!

> *(Enormous applause, stamping of feet. Sasha is standing, applauding with the rest. Anna and Vito leap onto the stage to grasp Emma's hand.)*

ANNA: Emma, the hall is full of federal agents!

VITO: They're coming down the aisle.

VOICE THROUGH MEGAPHONE: Clear the hall! By order of the United States government! No one leave the stage. Stay where you are.

> *(Vito turns toward the voice and gives it the arm. Then he takes Emma's hand on one side, Sasha's hand on the other. Anna takes Sasha's hand. The four face the audience as the lights go down.)*

END OF PLAY

MARX IN SOHO

A Play on History

PREFACE

I first read *The Communist Manifesto*—given to me, I am sure, by young Communists who lived in my working-class neighborhood—when I was about seventeen. It had a profound effect on me, because everything I saw in my own life, the lives of my parents, and the conditions in the United States in 1939, seemed to be explained, put into a historical context, and placed under a powerful analytical light.

I could see that my father, a Jewish immigrant from Austria, with but a fourth-grade education, worked very, very hard yet could barely support his wife and four sons. I could see that my mother worked day and night to make sure we were fed, clothed, and taken care of when we were sick. Their lives were an unending struggle for survival. I knew too that there were people in the nation who possessed astonishing wealth, and who certainly did not work as hard as my parents. The system was not fair.

All around me in that time of depression were families in desperate need through no fault of their own; unable to pay the rent, their belongings were thrown out on the street by the landlord, backed by the law. I knew from the newspapers that this was true all over the country.

I was a reader. I had read many of Dickens's novels since I was thirteen, and they had awakened within me an indignation against injustice, a compassion for people treated cruelly by their

employers, by the legal system. Now, in 1939, I read John Stein-
beck's *The Grapes of Wrath*, and that indignation returned, this
time directed at the rich and powerful in this country.

In the *Manifesto*, Karl Marx and Frederick Engels (Marx was
thirty, Engels twenty-eight, and Engels said later that Marx
was the principal writer) described what I was experiencing, what
I was reading about, which, I now saw, was not an aberration of
nineteenth-century England or depression-era America, but a
fundamental truth about the capitalist system. And this system,
deeply entrenched as it was in the modern world, was not eternal
—it had come into being at a certain stage of history, and one day
it would depart the scene, replaced by a socialist system. That was
an inspiring thought.

"The history of all hitherto existing society is the history
of class struggles," they proclaimed in the opening pages of the
Manifesto. So, the rich and the poor did not face each other as
individuals, but as classes. This made the conflict between them
something monumental. And it suggested that working people,
poor people, had something to bind them together in their quest
for justice—their common membership in the working class.

And what of the role of the government in that struggle of
the classes? "Equal justice for all" was carved on the facade of
public buildings. But in the *Manifesto*, Marx and Engels wrote:
"The executive of the modern state is but a committee for managing the common affairs of the whole bourgeoisie." They presented a startling idea: that the machinery of government was not
neutral, that, despite its pretensions, it served the capitalist class.

At the age of seventeen, I suddenly saw this idea dramatized.
My Communist friends brought me along with them to a demonstration in Times Square. Hundreds of people unfurled ban-
ners proclaiming opposition to war, opposition to fascism, and
marched along the street. I heard sirens. Mounted police charged
the crowd. I was knocked unconscious by a plainclothes policeman. When I came to, as my head was clearing, I could only think

one troubling thought: the police, the state, did the bidding of the holders of great wealth. How much freedom of speech and freedom of assembly you had depended on what class you were in.

When, at the age of eighteen, I went to work in a shipyard in Brooklyn as an apprentice shipfitter (our job was to fit together, with rivets, with welding, the steel plates of the hulls of battleships), I was already "class-conscious." In the shipyard, I found three other young workers like myself, and the four of us undertook to organize our fellow apprentices, who were excluded from the craft unions. We also agreed to meet weekly and read the works of Marx and Engels.

Thus I read Engels's exposition of Marxist philosophy in his book *Anti-Dühring* (a polemic against a writer named Dühring) and made my way laboriously through the first volume of *Das Kapital*. The system, I saw, with some excitement, was now laid bare. Behind all the complications of economic transactions, there were certain core truths: labor was the source of all value; labor produced a value beyond its meager wages; and that surplus value went into the pockets of the capitalist class. Capitalists needed unemployment—a "reserve army of labor"—to keep wages down. The system cherished things, especially money, more than people ("commodity fetishism"), so that everything good in life was measured by its exchange value.

Marxist theory explained that exploitation and class struggle were not new phenomena in world history, but that capitalism brought them to their sharpest point, and on a world scale. Capitalism was a progressive force in history at a certain stage of human development. "The bourgeoisie, historically, has played a most revolutionary part," they wrote in the *Manifesto*. It has enabled enormous technological and scientific progress, created huge wealth. But this became concentrated in fewer and fewer hands. There was a fundamental conflict between the increasingly organized forces of production and the anarchy of the market system. At some point, the exploited proletariat would organize, rebel, take power, and use the advanced technology for human need, not for the enrichment of the capitalist class.

That was my early introduction to Marx. Years later—after serving as a bombardier in the Eighth Air Force in World War II, and going to college and graduate school with the help of the G.I. Bill of Rights and the support of my wife and two children— I began to teach history and politics, first in the South, at Spelman College. After seven years at Spelman, I accepted a job at Boston University and moved north. In my courses in political theory, I paid serious attention to the writings of Marx and Engels.

At some point in the late 1960s, I became interested in anarchism, for several reasons. One was the growing evidence of the horrors of Stalinism in the Soviet Union, which suggested that the classical Marxian concept of "the dictatorship of the proletariat" needed to be reconsidered. Another was my own experience in the South in the struggle against racial segregation spearheaded by the Student Nonviolent Coordinating Committee. SNCC ("Snick," as it was called), without any self-conscious theorizing, acted in accord with anarchist principles: no central authority, grassroots democratic decision-making. In the New Left of the 1960s, this was called "participatory democracy."

I began to read about anarchism, beginning with the American anarchist-feminist Emma Goldman and her friend Alexander Berkman. I went on to Peter Kropotkin and Mikhail Bakunin. Bakunin was a fierce opponent of Marx's concept of how a revolution should come about. Emma Goldman, deported to Russia from the United States in 1919 for opposing World War I, observed that the new Soviet state was imprisoning not just its bourgeois opponents but dissident revolutionaries, and harshly criticized what she considered a betrayal of the socialist dream. This immersion in anarchist thought led me to initiate a seminar at Boston University on "Marxism and Anarchism."

From 1965 (the year of serious escalation of the war in Vietnam) to 1975 (when the Saigon government surrendered), I was heavily involved in the movement against the war, and my writings were very much concentrated on issues connected with the war. When the war ended, I felt free to do other things, and I wrote a play about Emma Goldman, *Emma,* which was performed in Boston and New York, and years later in London and Tokyo. In one of the play's scenes, young New York revolutionaries in a Lower East Side café argue about Marx's ideas versus Bakunin's.

I was very interested in the personal lives of these thinkers. Emma Goldman's autobiography, *Living My Life,* was a candid account of her tempestuous life as a rebel, not only in politics, but in sex. Marx never wrote an autobiography, but I could turn to a number of biographies for insights into his private life. In addition, there was a brilliant biography of his daughter Eleanor Marx by the English writer Yvonne Kapp, in which she recounts the details of the Marx family's life in London.

Karl and Jenny Marx had moved to London after he was expelled from country after country on the European continent. They lived in the grubby Soho district, and revolutionaries from all over Europe, arriving in London, trooped in and out of their home. The imagined scene—Marx at home, Marx with his wife, Jenny, with his daughter Eleanor—fascinated me.

My happy experience with the Emma Goldman play had lured me into the world of the theater, and I set out to write a play about Karl Marx. I wanted to show Marx as few people knew him, as a family man, struggling to support his wife and children. Three of the children had died very early, and three daughters survived.

I also wanted the audience to see Marx defending his ideas against attack. I knew his wife, Jenny, was a formidable thinker herself, and I imagined her confronting Marx from time to time. I knew that his daughter Eleanor was a precociously brilliant child, and I could see her challenging some of his most sophisticated theories. I wanted to subject Marx's ideas to an anarchist critique, and decided to invent a visit to his home by Bakunin. (In fact, there is no record of such a visit, although Marx and Bakunin knew one another and were fierce opponents inside the International Workingmen's Association, the First International.)

There was something else I thought missing from the usual appraisals of Marx. The emphasis was always on Marx the thinker, the theoretician. I knew that Marx was extraordinarily active as a revolutionary, first as a rebellious journalist in Germany, then with workers' associations in Paris and the Communist League in Brussels. He was active in the Rhineland during the European revolutions of 1848, which led to his trial and acquittal after a dramatic speech in court. After his exile to London, he was involved with the International Workingmen's Association, with the cause of Irish freedom, and in 1871 as a supporter of the Paris Commune.

His writings during these years were not only theoretical writings in political economy, as in *Das Kapital,* but immediate reactions to political events, to the 1848 revolutions, to the Commune of Paris, to workers' struggles all over the continent. I therefore wanted to put on stage this other side of Marx—the passionate, engaged revolutionary. The play I wrote included as characters Marx; his wife, Jenny; his daughter Eleanor; his friend Engels; and his political rival Bakunin. It had a reading in Boston that was well received, but which didn't satisfy me. I then set out to turn it into a one-person play.

My wife, Roslyn, always a perceptive critic of my writing, kept prodding me to make the play more directly relevant to our time, rather than a historical piece about Marx and Europe in the nineteenth century. I knew she was right about this and, after wrestling with it for a while, came up with the idea that Marx, in a kind of fantasy, would return from wherever he was to the present. Furthermore, he would return to the United States, so that he could not only reminisce about his life in nineteenth-century

Europe, but comment on what is happening here today. I decided I would have the authorities, whoever they are, return him, by bureaucratic error, not to Soho in London where he lived, but to Soho in New York.

Although it was a one-person play, I would have Marx bring to life, through his reminiscences, the important people in his life, especially his wife, Jenny, and his daughter Eleanor. And he would bring back Bakunin, the anarchist. All of them, in different ways, would be subjecting Marx's ideas to blunt criticism. There would be a dialectic of opposing viewpoints, presented through Marx's own recapturing of the arguments.

I wrote the play at a time when the collapse of the Soviet Union brought an almost universal exultation in the mainstream press and among political leaders: not only was "the enemy" gone, but the ideas of Marxism were discredited. Capitalism and the "free market" had triumphed. Marxism had failed. Marx was truly dead. I thought it important, therefore, to make it clear that neither the Soviet Union, nor other countries that called themselves "Marxist" but had set up police states, represented Marx's notion of socialism. I wanted to show Marx as angry that his theories had been so distorted as to stand for Stalinist cruelties. I thought it necessary to rescue Marx not only from those pseudosocialists who established repressive rule in various parts of the world, but also from all those writers and politicians in the West who now gloated over the triumph of capitalism.

Marx's critique of capitalism, I wanted to show, remains fundamentally true in our time. His analysis is corroborated every day in the newspaper headlines. He saw the unprecedented speed and chaos of technological change and social change in his time, which is even more true today. "Constant revolutionizing of production, uninterrupted disturbance of all social conditions, everlasting uncertainty and agitation distinguish the bourgeois epoch from all earlier ones. All fixed, fast-frozen relations, with their train of ancient and venerable prejudices and opinions, are swept away, all new-formed ones become antiquated before they can ossify. All that is solid melts into air." This was in the *Manifesto*.

What we speak of as "globalization" Marx saw very clearly. Again, the *Manifesto*: "The need of a constantly expanding market for its products chases the bourgeoisie over the whole surface of the globe. It must nestle everywhere, settle everywhere, establish connections everywhere. . . . In place of the old local and national seclusion and self-sufficiency, we have intercourse in every direction, universal interdependence of nations." The "free-trade agreements" sought by the United States government in recent years are attempts to remove whatever restrictions there are to the free flow of capital across the globe—giving capitalists the right to exploit people everywhere.

The headlines Marx looks at in the course of the play are not surprising to him. He saw the mergers of huge enterprises, which go on today, but on a larger scale. He saw the growing gap between the rich and the poor, which is true not just within each country but, even more dramatically, between the people of rich nations and those of poor nations.

In the play, Marx says that socialism should not take on the characteristics of capitalism. Observing how opponents of the regime have been put to death in pseudosocialist countries, he reflects on what he said about the system of crime and punishment when he was writing in the *New York Daily Tribune* in 1853: "Is there not a necessity for deeply reflecting upon the alteration of the system that breeds these crimes, instead of glorifying the hangman who executes a lot of criminals to make room only for the supply of new ones?"

We live in a society that Marx's phrase "commodity fetishism" perfectly describes. As Ralph Waldo Emerson put it, roughly around the same time, watching the beginning of the American industrial system: "Things are in the saddle and ride mankind."

The protection of corporate property is deemed more important than the protection of human life. Indeed, the Supreme Court decided in the late nineteenth century that a corporation was "a person" and so protected by the Fourteenth Amendment, more protected, in fact, than black people, for whom that amendment was originally written.

Marx was but twenty-five years old, living in Paris with Jenny, when he wrote a remarkable document, published only many years later, known as *The Economic and Philosophical Manuscripts*. Marx wrote there about alienation in the modern world, brought to its peak under capitalism, with human beings alienated from their labor, from nature, from one another, and from their own true selves. This is a phenomenon we see all around us in our time, one that results in psychological as well as material misery.

Marx devoted most of his writing to a critique of capitalism and very little to a description of what a socialist society might look like. But we can extrapolate from what he says about capitalism to imagine a society without exploitation, where people feel at one with nature, with the work they do, with each other, and with themselves. Marx gives us some clues about the future when he describes in glowing terms the society created by the Paris Commune of 1871 in the few short months of its existence. I tried to incorporate that vision in this play.

Those who read *Marx in Soho* may wonder how much is historically accurate. The major events in Marx's life and in the history of the era are fundamentally true: his marriage to Jenny, his exile to London, the death of his three children, and the political conflicts of the time: the Irish struggle against England, the 1848 revolutions in Europe, the Communist movement, the Paris Commune. The main characters he talks about are real: the members of his family, his friend Engels, his rival Bakunin. The dialogue is invented, but I have tried to be true to the personalities and the thinking of the characters, though I may be taking some liberties in imagining his ideological conflicts with Jenny and Eleanor. On a few occasions, as in his description of Napoleon III, I use Marx's own words.

My hope is that *Marx in Soho* illuminates not just that time, and Marx's place in it, but our time, and our place in it.

MARX IN SOHO

A Play on History

House lights up part of the way. Light on center stage, showing a bare stage, except for a table and several chairs. Marx enters, wearing a black frock coat and vest, white shirt, black floppy tie. He is bearded, short, stocky, with a black mustache and hair turning gray, wearing steel-rimmed spectacles. He is carrying a draw-sack, stops, walks to the edge of the stage, looks out at the audience, and seems pleased, a little surprised.

Thank God, an audience!

> *(He unloads his supplies from the draw-sack: a few books, newspapers, a bottle of beer, a glass. He turns and walks to the front of the stage.)*

Good of you to come. You weren't put off by all those idiots who said: "Marx is dead!" Well, I am . . . and I am not. That's dialectics for you.

> *(He doesn't mind joking about himself or his ideas. Perhaps he's mellowed over all these years. But just when you think Marx has grown soft, there are bursts of anger.)*

You may wonder how I got here. . . . *(Smiles mischievously)* . . . Public transportation.

> *(His accent is slightly British, slightly continental, nothing to draw attention, but definitely not American.)*

I did not expect to come back *here*. . . . I wanted to return to Soho.

That's where I lived in London. But . . . a bureaucratic mix-up. Here I am, Soho in New York. . . . *(Sighs)* Well, I always wanted to visit New York. *(Pours himself some beer, takes a drink, puts it down)*

> *(His mood changes.)*

Why have I returned?

> *(He shows a little anger.)*

To clear my name!

> *(He lets that sink in.)*

I've been reading your newspapers. . . . *(Picks up a newspaper)* They are all proclaiming that my ideas are dead! It's nothing new. These clowns have been saying this for more than a hundred years. Don't you wonder: why is it necessary to declare me dead again and again?

Well, I have had it up to here. I asked for the right to come back, just for a while. But there are rules. I told you: it's a bureaucracy. It is permissible to read, even to watch. But not to travel. I protested, of course. And had some support . . . Socrates told them: "The untraveled life is not worth living!" Gandhi fasted. Mother Jones threatened to picket. Mark Twain came to my defense, in his own strange way. Buddha chanted: Ommmm! But the others kept quiet. My God, at this point, what do they have to lose?

Yes, there too I have a reputation as a troublemaker. And even there, protest works! Finally, they said, "All right, you can go. You can have an hour or so to speak your mind. But remember, *no agitating!*" They do believe in freedom of speech . . . but within limits. . . . *(Smiles)* They are liberals.

You can spread the word: Marx is back! For a short while. But understand one thing—I'm not a Marxist. *(Laughs)* I said that once to Pieper and he almost croaked. I should tell you about Pieper. *(Takes a drink of beer)*

We were living in London. Jenny and I and the little ones.

Plus two dogs, three cats, and two birds. Barely living. A flat on Dean Street, near where they dumped the city's sewage. We were in London because I had been expelled from the continent. Expelled from the Rhineland, yes, from my birthplace.

I had done dangerous things. I was editor of a newspaper, *Der Rheinische Zeitung*. Hardly revolutionary. But I suppose the most revolutionary act one can engage in is . . . to tell the truth.

In the Rhineland, the police were arresting poor people for gathering firewood from the estates of the rich. I wrote an editorial protesting that. Then they tried to censor our paper. I wrote an editorial declaring that there was no freedom of the press in Germany. They decided to prove me right. They shut us down. Only then did we become radical—isn't that the way it is? Our last issue of the *Zeitung* had a huge headline in red ink: "Revolt!" . . . That annoyed the authorities. They ordered me out of the Rhineland.

So, I went to Paris. Where else do exiles go? Where else can you sit all night in a café and tell lies about how revolutionary you were in the old country? . . . Yes, if you are going to be an exile, be one in Paris.

Paris was our honeymoon. Jenny found a tiny flat in the Latin Quarter. Heavenly months. But the word was out, from the German police to the Paris police. It seems that the police develop an internationalist consciousness long before the workers. . . . So, I was expelled from Paris, too. We went to Belgium. Expelled again.

We came to London, where refugees come from all over the world. The English are admirable in their tolerance . . . and insufferable in their boasting about it.

> (*He coughs, which he will do from time to time. Shakes his head*)

The doctors told me the cough would go away in a few weeks. That was in 1858.

But I was telling you about Pieper. You see, in London, the political refugees from the continent marched in and out of our house. Pieper was one of them. He buzzed around me like a hornet. He was a flatterer, a sycophant. He would station himself six inches from me, to make sure I could not evade him, and he would quote from my writings. I would say: "Pieper, please don't quote me to myself."

He had the audacity to say, thinking I would be pleased, that he would translate *Das Kapital* into English. Ha! The man could not speak an English sentence without butchering it. English is a beautiful language. It is Shakespeare's language. If Shakespeare had heard Pieper speak one sentence of English, he would have taken poison!

But Jenny felt sorry for him. She liked to invite him to our family dinners. One evening, Pieper came and announced the formation of "The Marxist Society of London."

"A Marxist society?" I asked. "What's that?"

"We meet every week to discuss another of your writings. We read aloud, examine sentence by sentence. That's why we call ourselves Marxists—we believe completely and wholeheartedly in everything you have written."

"Completely and wholeheartedly?" I asked.

"Yes, and we would be honored, Herr Doktor Marx"—he always called me Herr Doktor Marx—"if you would address the next meeting of the Marxist society."

"I cannot do that."

"Why?" he asked.

"Because *I am not a Marxist*." *(Laughs heartily)*

I didn't mind his bad English. Mine was not that perfect. It was his way of thinking. He was an embarrassment, a satellite encircling my words, reflecting them to the world but distorting them. And then he defended the distortions like a fanatic, denouncing anyone who interpreted them differently.

I once said to Jenny: "Do you know what I fear most?"

And she said: "That the workers' revolution will never come?"

"No, that the revolution *will* come, and it will be taken over by men like Pieper—flatterers when out of power, bullies and braggarts when holding power. Dogmatists. They will speak for the proletariat and they will interpret my ideas for the world. They will organize a new priesthood, a new hierarchy, with excommunications and indexes, inquisitions and firing squads.

"All this will be done in the name of Communism, delaying for a hundred years the Communism of freedom, dividing the world between capitalist empires and Communist empires. They will muck up our beautiful dream and it will take another revolution, maybe two or three, to clean it up. That's what I fear."

No, I wasn't going to have Pieper translate *Das Kapital* into English. It represented fifteen years of work—in the conditions of Soho. Walking every morning past beggars sleeping amidst the sewage, making my way to the British Museum and its magnificent library, working there until dusk, reading, reading . . . Is there anything more dull than reading political economy? *(He thinks.)* Yes, writing political economy.

Then, home through the darkening streets, listening to the vendors calling out the prices of their wares, and the veterans of the Crimean War, some blind, others without legs, begging for a penny in the noxious air. . . . The poor-smell of London, yes.

My critics, trying to minimize what went into *Das Kapital,* would say, as they always say about radical writers, "Oh, he must have had some dreadful personal experience." Yes, if you want to make much of it, that walk home through Soho fueled the anger that went into *Das Kapital.*

I hear you saying, "Well, of course, that's how it was *then,* a century ago." Only *then?* On my way here today, I walked through the streets of your city, surrounded by garbage, breathing foul air, past the bodies of men and women sleeping on the street, huddled against the cold. Instead of a lassie singing a ballad, I heard a voice in my ear ... *plaintively:* "Some change, sir, for a cup of coffee?"

(Angry now) You call this progress, because you have motor cars and telephones and flying machines and a thousand potions to make you smell better? And people sleeping on the streets?

(He picks up a newspaper and peers at it.) An official report: the United States' Gross National Product (yes, gross!) last year was seven thousand billion dollars. Most impressive. But tell me, where is it? Who is profiting from it? Who is not? *(Reads from the newspaper again)* Less than five hundred individuals control two thousand billion dollars in business assets. Are these people more noble, more hard working, more valuable to society than the mother in the tenement, nurturing three children through the winter, with no money to pay the heating bill?

Did I not say, a hundred and fifty years ago, that capitalism would enormously increase the wealth of society, but that this wealth would be concentrated in fewer and fewer hands? *(Reads from newspaper)* "Giant merger of Chemical Bank and Chase Manhattan Bank. Twelve thousand workers will lose jobs. . . . Stocks rise." And they say my ideas are dead!

Do you know Oliver Goldsmith's poem "The Deserted Village"?

(Recites) "Ill fares the land to hastening ills a prey / Where wealth accumulates and men decay." Yes, *decay.* That's what I saw as I walked through your city this morning. Houses decaying, schools decaying, human beings decaying. But then I walked a bit farther, and I was suddenly surrounded by men of obvious wealth, women in jewels and furs. Suddenly I heard the sound of sirens. Was violence being done somewhere nearby? Was a crime being committed? Was someone trying to take part of the Gross National Product, illegally, from those who had stolen it legally? Ah, the wonders of the market system! Human beings reduced

to commodities, their lives controlled by the super-commodity, money.

(Lights flash threateningly. Marx looks up, confides to audience)
The committee doesn't like that!

(His tone softens, reminiscing.) In that little flat in Soho, Jenny made hot soup and boiled potatoes. There was fresh bread from our friend the baker down the street. We would sit around the table and eat and talk about events of the day—the Irish struggle for freedom, the latest war, the stupidity of the country's leaders, a political opposition confining itself to pips and squeaks, the cowardly press. . . . I suppose things are different these days, eh?

After dinner, we would clear the table and I would work. With my cigars handy, and a glass of beer. Yes, work until three or four in the morning. My books piled up on one side, the parliamentary reports piled up on another. Jenny would be at the other end of the table, transcribing—my handwriting was impossible, and she would rewrite every word of mine—can you imagine a more heroic act?

Occasionally, a crisis. No, not a world crisis. A book would be missing. One day I could not find my Ricardo. I asked Jenny: "Where is my Ricardo?"

"You mean *Principles of Political Economy?*" Well, she thought I was finished with it and she had taken it to the pawnshop.

I lost my temper. "My Ricardo! You pawned my Ricardo!"

She said: "Be quiet! Last week didn't we pawn the ring my mother gave me?"

That's how it was. *(Sighs)* We pawned everything. Especially gifts from Jenny's family. When we ran out of those gifts, we pawned our clothes. One winter—do you know the London winters?—I did without my overcoat. Another time, I walked out of the house and my feet began to freeze on the snow, and then I realized: I was not wearing shoes. We had pawned them the day before.

When *Das Kapital* was published, we celebrated, but Engels had to give us some money so we could go to the pawnshop and retrieve our linens and dishes for the dinner. Engels . . . a saint. There's no other word for him. When they cut off our water, our gas, and the house was dark, our spirits low, Engels paid the bills. His father owned factories in Manchester. Yes . . . *(smiling)* . . . capitalism saved us!

He did not always understand our needs. We had no money for groceries and he would send us crates of wine! One Christmas, when we had no means to buy a *Weihnachtsbaum*— a Christmas tree—Engels arrived with six bottles of champagne. So, we imagined a tree, formed a circle around it, drank champagne, and sang Christmas songs. *(Marx sings, hums a snatch of a Christmas carol)* "Tannenbaum . . ."

I knew what my revolutionary friends were thinking: Marx, the atheist, with a Christmas tree!

Yes, I did describe religion as the opium of the people, but no one has ever paid attention to the full passage. Listen. *(He picks up a book and reads.)* "Religion is the sigh of the oppressed creature, the heart of a heartless world, the soul of soulless conditions, it is the opium of the people." True, opium is no solution, but it may be necessary to relieve pain. *(Shakes his head)* Don't I know that from my boils? And doesn't the world have a terrible case of boils?

I keep thinking about Jenny. *(He stops, rubs his eyes.)* How she packed all our possessions and brought our two girls, Jennichen and Laura, across the Channel to London. And then gave birth three times in our miserable cold flat on Dean Street. Nursed those babies and tried to keep them warm. And saw them die one by one. . . . Guido, he had not even begun to walk. And Francesca, she was one year old. . . . I had to borrow three pounds to pay for her coffin. . . . As for Moosh, he lived for eight years, but something was wrong from the start. He had a large handsome head, but the rest of him never grew. The night he died, we all slept on the floor around his body until the morning came.

When Eleanor was born, we were fearful. But she was a tough little thing. It was good that she had two older sisters. They had barely survived themselves. Jennichen was born in Paris. Paris is marvelous for lovers, but not for children. Something about the air. Laura was our second, born in Brussels. No one should be born in Brussels.

In London, we had no money. But we always had Sunday picnics. We would walk an hour and a half into the countryside, Jenny and I, the children, and Lenchen (oh, I'll tell you about her . . .). Lenchen would make a roast veal. And we would have tea, fruit, bread, cheese, beer. Eleanor was the youngest, but she drank beer.

No money, but children need a vacation. Once, I took the rent money and sent them to the Atlantic coast of France. Another time, with our groceries money, I bought a piano, because the girls loved music.

A father is not supposed to have favorites among his children. But Eleanor! I would say to Jenny: "Eleanor is a strange child." And Jenny would reply: "You expect the children of Karl Marx to be normal?"

Eleanor was the youngest, the brightest. Imagine a revolutionary at the age of eight. That's how old she was in 1863. Poland was in rebellion against Russian rule, and Tussy wrote a letter (that's what we called her: Tussy)—she wrote to Engels about "those brave little fellows in Poland," as she called them. When she was nine, she sent a letter to America, advice to President Lincoln, telling him how to win the war against the Confederacy!

Also, she smoked. And drank wine. Still, she was a child. She would dress her dolls . . . while sipping from a glass of wine! She played chess with me when she was ten, and I could not easily defeat her. At fifteen, she suddenly became furious against the law about observing the Lord's Day. No activity on Sunday was permitted. So, she organized "Sunday Evenings for the People" at St. Martin's Hall, brought musicians there to play Handel, Mozart, Beethoven. The hall was packed. Two thousand people. It was illegal, but no one was arrested. A lesson. If you are going to break the law, do it with two thousand people . . . and Mozart.

I used to read Shakespeare and Aeschylus and Dante aloud to her and her sisters, which she loved. Her room was a Shakespeare museum. She memorized *Romeo and Juliet* and insisted that I read, over and over, those lines of Romeo, when he sees Juliet for the first time:

> The brightness of her cheek would shame those stars
> As daylight doth a lamp; her eyes in heaven
> Would through the airy region stream so bright
> That birds would sing and think it were not night.

Tussy was not easy to live with. Oh, no! Do you know how embarrassing it is to have a child who finds flaws in your reasoning? She would argue with me about my writings! For instance, my essay "On the Jewish Question." Not easy to understand, I admit. Well, Eleanor read it, and immediately challenged me: "Why do you single out the Jews as representatives of capitalism? They are not the only ones poisoned by commerce and greed."

I tried to explain: I wasn't singling out the Jews, just using them as a vivid example. Her answer was to start wearing a Jewish star. "I'm a Jew," she announced. What could I say? I shrugged my shoulders and Eleanor said: *"That's a very Jewish gesture."* She could be very annoying!

Tussy knew my father had converted to Christianity. It was not practical to be a Jew in Germany. . . . Is it ever practical to be a Jew, anywhere? He had me baptized at the age of eight. This fact intrigued Eleanor. She asked: "Moor"—the family called me

Moor because of my dark complexion—"I know you were baptized. But first you were circumcised, weren't you?" Nothing embarrassed that girl!

At such times she was impossible. Listen to this. Alongside
her Jewish star, she wore her crucifix. No, she was not enamored
of Christianity, but of the Irish, and their rebellion against England. She learned about the Irish struggle from Lizzie Burns,
Engels' love.

Lizzie was a mill girl and could not read. Engels spoke nine
languages. You might think this would make it hard for them to
communicate. But they loved one another. Lizzie was active in
the Irish movement. Tussy would visit and the two of them would
sit on the floor and drink wine together and sing Irish songs until
they fell asleep.

There was that terrible night, the night the English government hanged two young Irishmen, right there in Soho, with
a drunken crowd cheering. . . . Those genteel English with their
afternoon tea and their public hangings! I understand you don't
hang people anymore—only gas them, or inject poison into their
veins, or use electricity to burn them to death. Much more civilized. Yes, they hanged two young Irishmen for wanting freedom
from England. Eleanor wept and wept.

I would say to her: "Tussy, you don't have to get involved
so soon with the horrors of the world. You're fifteen." And she
would answer: "That's the point, Moor. I'm not thirteen. I'm not
fourteen. I'm *fifteen*."

Yes, she was fifteen, and she became infatuated with any
dashing, handsome man who visited our flat. I could draw up a
list. For all the rest of her life, Eleanor was clever in politics, idi-
otic in love. She was mad about the hero of the Paris Commune,
Lissagaray. Well, at least he was a Frenchman.

Jennichen's fellow was English. English men are like English
food. Need I say more? And there was Laura's lover, LaFargue.

His public displays of ardor were absurd. He would put his hand on her ass, in public, as if it were the most natural thing. And Jenny defended him. "It's his Creole background," she said. "You know his family came to France from Cuba." As if in Cuba everyone went around with their hands on somebody's ass!

(Sighs) Jenny was always trying to calm me down. Well, she might calm me, but she was unsuccessful with my boils. *(Grimaces)* Did you ever have boils? There is no sickness more odious. They plagued me all my life. And led to stupid attempts to analyze me via my boils. "Marx is angry at the capitalist system because he has boils!" What imbeciles! How do they account for all the revolutionaries who don't have boils?

Of course, they always find something: this one was beaten by his father; this one was nursed by his mother until he was ten; that one had no toilet training—as if one must be abnormal to resent exploitation. Every explanation except the obvious one, that capitalism, by its nature, its attack on the human spirit, breeds rebellion. . . .

Oh yes, they say capitalism has become more humane since my time. Really? Just a few years ago—it was in the newspapers —factory owners locked the doors on the women in their chicken factory in North Carolina. Why? To make more profit. There was a fire, and twenty-five workers were trapped, burned to death.

Perhaps my anger did inflame my boils. But try working, try sitting and writing, with boils on your ass! And don't tell me about doctors. The doctors knew less than I did. Much less, because the boils were mine. *(Takes another drink of beer)*

I could not sleep. Then I discovered something miraculous —water. Yes, as simple as that. Cloths soaked in warm water. Jenny would apply them patiently, hour after hour. She would wake up in the middle of the night when I cried out, and apply those soothing wet cloths. . . . Sometimes, when Jenny was away, Lenchen would do that.

(He stops to reflect.) Yes, Lenchen. Here we are, living in poverty in Soho, and Jenny's mother decides to send us Lenchen, to help with the babies. We had pawned our furniture, but suddenly we had a servant girl. That's how it is when you marry into aristocracy. Your in-laws don't send you money, which you desperately need. They send you fine linens and silverware. And a servant. Actually, not a bad idea. The servant can take the linens and silverware to the pawnshop and get some money. Lenchen did that many times. . . .

But she was never a servant. The children adored her. And Jenny had tremendous affection for her. When Jenny was ill, Lenchen was with her, tending to every need.

But, yes, her presence created a great tension between Jenny and me. I remember a scene. Jenny said: "This morning, I saw you looking at Lenchen."

"Looking? What do you mean?"

"I mean the way a man looks at a woman."

"I still don't know what you mean." *(Shakes his head sadly)* It was one of those conversations which cannot possibly come to any good.

There was all this going on inside our flat on Dean Street. And outside was London. . . . Can you imagine the streets of London in 1858? The coster girls, trying to sell a few rolls for a few pennies. The organ grinder with his monkey. The prostitutes, the magicians, the fire-eaters, the street vendors bellowing trumpets, ringing bells, the hurdy-gurdies, the organs, the brass bands, the fiddlers, the Scottish pipers, and always a beggar girl singing an Irish ballad. That's what I saw and heard, walking home every evening from the British Museum, under the gas lamps that had just been lit, until I got to Dean Street and made my way through the mud and sewage, thinking about the care they took in paving streets of the wealthy neighborhoods. *(Sighs)* Well, I suppose it was only fitting that the author of *Das Kapital* should slog through shit while writing his condemnation of the capitalist system. . . .

Jenny did not sympathize with my complaints about wading through the mud on the street. She would say: "That's how it feels to me reading *Das Kapital!*" She was always my severest critic. Unsparing. Honest, you might say. Is there anything more outrageous than an honest critic?

The book troubled her. Yes, *Das Kapital. (Picks up the book)* She worried that I would bore people from the start with my discussion of commodities, use value, exchange value. She said the book was too long, too detailed. She used the word "ponderous." Imagine!

She reminded me what our trade union friend Peter Fox said when I gave him the book. "I feel like a man who has been given an elephant as a gift."

Yes, Jenny said, it *is* an elephant. I tried to tell her this is not *The Communist Manifesto,* which was intended for the general public. It is an analysis.

"Let it be an analysis," she said. "But let it cry out like the *Manifesto.*"

"*A spectre is haunting Europe—the spectre of Communism!* Yes," she said, "that excites the reader. . . . *A spectre is haunting Europe!*"

And then she read to me the first words of *Das Kapital,* to torment me, of course. *(Marx picks the book from the table and reads.)* "The wealth of those societies in which the capitalist mode of production prevails presents itself as an immense accumulation of commodities."

She said, "That will put readers to sleep."

I ask you, Is that boring? *(He thinks.)* Maybe it is a little boring. I admitted that to Jenny. She said, "There's no such thing as *a little* boring."

Don't misunderstand. She did see *Das Kapital* as a profound analysis. It showed how the capitalist system must, at a certain stage in history, come into being and bring about a colossal growth of the productive forces, an unprecedented increase in the wealth of the world. And then how it must, by its own nature, distribute that wealth in such a way as to destroy the humanity of both laborer and capitalist. And how it must, by its nature, create its own gravediggers and give way to a more human system.

But Jenny always asked, "Are we reaching the people we want to reach?"

One day, she said to me: "Do you know why the censors have allowed it to be published? Because they cannot understand it and assume no one else will."

I reminded her that *Das Kapital* was receiving favorable reviews. She reminded me that most of the reviews were written by Engels. . . . I told her that perhaps she was being critical of my work because she was unhappy with me.

"You men!" she said. "You cannot believe that your work *deserves* criticism and so you attribute it to something personal. Yes, Moor, my personal feelings are there, but this is separate."

Yes, her personal feelings. Jenny was having a terrible time then. I suppose I was responsible. But I did not know how to ease her anguish. You must understand, Jenny and I fell in love when I was seventeen and she was nineteen. She was marvelous-looking, with auburn hair and dark eyes. For some reason, her family took a liking to me. They were aristocrats. Aristocrats are always impressed with intellectuals. Jenny's father and I would have long discussions about Greek philosophy. I had done my doctoral thesis on Democritus and Heraclitus. I was beginning to realize that up to now the philosophers had only interpreted the world. But the point was to *change* it!

When I was expelled from Germany, Jenny followed me to Paris and there we married and she gave birth to Jennichen and Laura. We were happy in Paris, living on nothing, meeting our friends in a café. They also lived on nothing. What a bunch we were! Bakunin, the huge, shaggy anarchist. Engels, the handsome atheist. Heine, the saintly poet. Oh, Stirner, the total misfit. And Proudhon, who said, "Property is theft!" . . . but wanted some!

Being poor in Paris is one thing. Being poor in London is another. We moved there with two children, and soon Jenny was pregnant again. Sometimes I felt she blamed me for having to bring up our children in a cold, damp flat where someone was sick all the time.

Jenny came down with smallpox. She recovered, but it left pockmarks on her face. I tried to tell her she was still beautiful, but it didn't help.

I wish you could know Jenny. What she did for me cannot be calculated. And she accepted the fact that I could not simply get a job like other men. Yes, I did try once. I wrote a letter of inquiry to the railway for a position as clerk. They responded as follows: "Dr. Marx, we are honored with your request for a position here. We have never had a doctor of philosophy working for us as a clerk. But the position requires a legible handwriting, so we must regretfully decline your offer." *(He shrugs.)*

Jenny believed in my ideas. But she was impatient with what she considered the pretensions of high-level scholarship. "Come down to earth, Herr Doktor," she would say.

She wanted me to describe the theory of surplus value so ordinary workers could understand it. I told her, "No one can understand it without first understanding the labor theory of value, and how labor power is a special commodity whose value is determined by the cost of the means of subsistence and yet gives value to all other commodities, a value which always exceeds the value of labor power."

She would shake her head: "No, that won't do. All you have to say is this: your employer gives you the barest amount in wages, just enough for you to survive and work; but out of your labor he makes far more than what he pays you. And so he gets richer and richer, while you stay poor."

All right, let us say only a hundred people in world history have ever understood my theory of surplus value. *(Gets heated)* But it is still true! Just last week, I was reading the reports of the United States Department of Labor. There you have it. Your workers are producing more and more goods and getting less and less in wages. What is the result? Just as I predicted. Now the richest one percent of the American population owns forty percent of the nation's wealth. And this in the great model of world capitalism, the nation that has not only robbed its own people, but sucked in the wealth of the rest of the world . . .

Jenny was always trying to simplify ideas that were, by their nature, complex. She accused me of being a scholar first and a revolutionary second. She said: "Forget your intellectual readers. Address the workers."

She called me arrogant and intolerant. "Why do you attack other revolutionaries more vehemently than you attack the bourgeoisie?" she asked.

Proudhon, for instance. The man did not understand that we must applaud capitalism for its development of giant industries, and then take them over. Proudhon thought we must retreat into a more simple society. When he wrote his book *The Philosophy of Poverty*, I replied with my own book, *The Poverty of Philosophy*. I thought this was clever. Jenny thought it was insulting. *(Sighs)* I suppose Jenny was a far better human being than I could ever be.

She encouraged me to get off my behind and get involved in the cause of the London workers. She came with me when I was invited to address the first meeting of the International Working Men's Association. It was the fall of 1864. Two thousand people were packed into St. Martin's Hall.

(Steps forward, extends his arm as if to a great crowd as he speaks very deliberately, powerfully) "The workers of all countries must unite against foreign policies which are criminal, which play upon national prejudices, which squander, in wars, the people's blood and treasure. We must combine across national boundaries to vindicate the simple laws of morals and justice in international affairs. . . . Workers of the world, unite!" Pauses.

Jenny liked that. . . . *(Takes a drink)*

She kept the family going, with the water cut off, the gas cut off. But she never tired of the subject of female emancipation. She said that the vitality of women was being sapped by staying at home and darning socks and cooking. And so she refused to stay at home.

She accused me of being theoretically an emancipationist but practically ignorant of the problems of women. "You and Engels," she said, "write about sexual equality, but you do not practice it." Well, I won't comment on that. . . .

She supported with all her heart the Irish struggle against England. Queen Victoria had said, "These Irish are really abominable people—not like any other civilized nation." Jenny wrote a letter to the London newspapers: "England hangs Irish rebels, who wanted nothing but freedom. Is England a civilized nation?"

Jenny and I were powerfully in love. How can I make you understand that? But we went through hellish times in London. The love was still there. But, at a certain point, things changed. I don't know why. Jenny said it was because she was no longer the great beauty I had wooed. That made me angry. She said it was because of Lenchen. That made me even more angry. She said I was angry because it was true. That made me furious!

(He sighs, takes a swallow of beer, looks over the newspapers on the table, picks one up.) They claim that because the Soviet Union collapsed, Communism is dead. *(Shakes his head)* Do these idiots

know what Communism is? Do they think that a system run by a thug who murders his fellow revolutionaries is Communism? *Scheisskopfen!*

Journalists, politicians who say such things—what kind of education did they have? Did they ever read the *Manifesto* that Engels and I wrote when he was twenty-eight years old and I was thirty?

(He reaches for a book on the table and reads.) "In place of the old bourgeois society, with its classes and class antagonisms, we shall have an association, in which the free development of each is the condition for the free development of all." Do you hear that? An association! Do they understand the objective of Communism? Freedom of the individual! To develop himself, herself, as a compassionate human being. Do they think that someone who calls himself a Communist or a socialist and acts like a gangster understands what Communism is?

To shoot those who disagree with you—can that be the Communism that I gave my life for? That monster who took all power for himself in Russia—and who insisted on interpreting my ideas like a religious fanatic—when he was putting his old comrades up against the wall before firing squads, did he allow his citizens to read that letter I wrote to the *New York Tribune* in which I said that capital punishment could not be justified in any society calling itself civilized? ... *(Angry)* Socialism is not supposed to reproduce the stupidities of capitalism!

Here in America, your prisons are crowded. Who is in them? The poor. Some of them have committed violent and terrible crimes. Most of them are burglars, thieves, robbers, sellers of drugs. They believe in free enterprise! They do what the capitalists do, but on a much smaller scale....

(He picks up another book.) Do you know what Engels and I wrote about prisons? "Rather than punishing individuals for their crimes, we should destroy the social conditions which engender

crime, and give to each individual the scope which he needs in society in order to develop his life."

Oh, yes, we spoke of a "dictatorship of the proletariat." Not a dictatorship of a *party*, of a central committee, not a dictatorship of one man. No, we spoke of a temporary dictatorship of the working class. The mass of the people would take over the state and govern in the interests of all—until the state itself would become unnecessary and gradually disappear.

Bakunin, of course, disagreed. He said that a state, even a workers' state, if it has an army, police, prisons, will become a tyranny. He loved to argue with me.

Do you know about him? Bakunin, the anarchist? If a novelist invented such a character, you would say the existence of such a person is not possible. To say Bakunin and I did not get along is a great understatement.

Listen to what he said at the time Engels and I were in Brussels, writing the *Manifesto. (Marx picks up a document from the table and reads.)* "Marx and Engels, especially Marx, are ingrained bourgeois."

We were ingrained bourgeois! Of course, compared to Bakunin, everyone was bourgeois, because Bakunin chose to live like a pig. And if you did not live like a pig, if you had a roof over your head, if you had a piano in your sitting room, if you enjoyed some fresh bread and wine, you were a bourgeois.

I grant the man courage. He was imprisoned, sent to Siberia, escaped, wandered the world trying to foment revolution everywhere. He wanted an anarchist society, but the only anarchism he ever succeeded in establishing was in his head. He tried to start an uprising in Bologna, and almost killed himself with his own revolver. His revolutions failed everywhere, but he was like a man whose failure with women only spurs him on to more.

Did you ever see a photograph of Bakunin? A giant of a man. Bald head, which he covered with a little gray cap. Massive beard.

Ferocious expression. He had no teeth—scurvy, the result of his prison diet. He seemed to live not in this world but in some world of his imagination. He was oblivious to money. When he had it, he gave it away; when he didn't have it, he borrowed without any thought of returning it. He had no home, or, you might say, the world was his home. He would arrive at a comrade's house and announce: "I'm here—where do I sleep? And what is there to eat?" In an hour he was more at home than his hosts!

There was that time in Soho. We were having dinner, and Bakunin burst in. Didn't bother to knock. It was his habit to arrive at dinnertime. We were surprised; we thought he was in Italy. Whenever we heard about him, he was in some far-off country organizing a revolution. Well, he almost knocked the door off its hinges, came in, looked around, smiled his toothless smile, and said, "Good evening, comrades." And without waiting for a response, sat down at the table, and began devouring sausage and meat in enormous chunks, stuffing in cheese, too, and glass after glass of brandy.

I said to him: "Mikhail, try the wine, we have plenty of that; brandy is expensive."

He drank some wine, spit it right out. "Absolutely tasteless," he said. "Brandy helps you think more clearly."

He then began his usual performance, preaching, arguing, ordering, shouting, exhorting. I was furious, but it was Jenny who spoke up. "Mikhail," she said, "Stop! You're consuming all the oxygen in the room!" He just roared with laughter and went on.

Bakunin's head was full of anarchist garbage, romantic, utopian nonsense. I wanted to expel him from the International. Jenny thought this ridiculous. Why, she asked, do revolutionary groups with six members always threaten someone with expulsion?

He had a hundred disguises, because the police were looking for him in every country in Europe. When he came to us in

London, he was disguised as a priest. At least he thought so. He looked ridiculous!

Well, he was with us a week. Once we stayed up the whole night, drinking and arguing and drinking some more, until neither of us could walk. In fact, I fell asleep in the midst of one of Bakunin's perorations. He shook me until I woke up, saying, "I haven't finished my point."

It was that glorious time in the winter of 1871, when the commune had taken power in Paris. . . . Yes, the Paris Commune. Bakunin leaped, with his full bulk, into that revolution. The French understood him. They had a saying: "On the first day of a revolution, Bakunin is a treasure. On the second day, he should be shot."

Do you know about that magnificent episode in human history, the Paris Commune? The story starts with stupidity. I am speaking of Napoleon the Third. Yes, the nephew of Bonaparte.

He was a buffoon, a stage actor smiling to the crowd while sixteen million French peasants lived in blind dark hovels, their children dying of starvation. But because he kept a legislature, because people voted, it was thought they had democracy. . . . A common mistake.

Bonaparte wanted glory, so he made the mistake of attacking Bismarck's armies. He was quickly defeated, whereupon the victorious German troops marched into Paris and were greeted by something more devastating than guns—silence. They found the statues of Paris draped in black, an immense, invisible, silent resistance. They did the wise thing. They paraded through the Arc de Triomphe and quickly departed.

And the old French order, the Republic. Liberals, they called themselves. They did not dare come into Paris. They were trembling with fear because, with the Germans gone, Paris was now taken over by the workers, the housewives, the clerks, the intellectuals, the armed citizens. The people of Paris formed not a government, but something more glorious, something governments everywhere fear, a commune, the collective energy of the people. It was the *Commune de Paris!*

People meeting twenty-four hours a day, all over the city, in knots of three and four, making decisions together, while the city was encircled by the French army, threatening to invade at any moment. Paris became the first free city of the world, the first enclave of liberty in a world of tyranny.

I said to Bakunin: "You want to know what I mean by the dictatorship of the proletariat? Look at the Commune of Paris. That is true democracy." Not the democracy of England or America, where elections are circuses, with people voting for one or another guardian of the old order, where whatever candidate wins, the rich go on ruling the country.

The Commune of Paris. It lived only a few months. But it was the first legislative body in history to represent the poor. Its laws were for them. It abolished their debts, postponed their rents, forced the pawnshops to return their most needed possessions. They refused to take salaries higher than the workers. They lowered the hours of bakers. And planned how to give free admission to the theater for everyone.

The great Courbet himself, whose paintings had stunned Europe, presided over the federation of artists. They reopened the museums, set up a commission for the education of women —something unheard of—education for women. They took advantage of the latest in science, the lighter-than-air balloon, and launched one out of Paris to soar over the countryside, dropping printed papers for the peasants, with a simple, powerful message, the message that should be dropped to working people everywhere in the world: "*Our interests are the same.*"

The commune declared the purpose of the schools—to teach children to love and respect their fellow creatures. I have read your endless discussions of education. Such nonsense! They teach everything needed to succeed in the capitalist world. But do they teach the young to struggle for justice?

The Communards understood the importance of that. They educated not only by their words, but by their acts. They destroyed the guillotine, that instrument of tyranny, even of revolutionary tyranny. Then, wearing red scarves, carrying a huge red banner, the buildings festooned with sheets of red silk, they gathered around the Vendôme Column, symbol of military power, a huge statue surmounted by the bronze head of Napoleon Bonaparte. A pulley was attached to the head, a capstan turned, and the head crashed to the ground. People climbed on the ruins. A red flag now floated from the pedestal. Now it was the pedestal not of one country but of the human race, and men and women, watching, wept with joy.

Yes, that was the Commune of Paris. The streets were always full, discussions going on everywhere. People shared things. They seemed to smile more often. Kindness ruled. The streets were safe, without police of any kind. Yes, *that* was socialism!

Of course that example, the example of the commune, could not be allowed. And so the armies of the Republic marched into Paris and commenced a slaughter. The leaders of the commune were taken to Père Lachaise Cemetery, put against the stone wall, and shot. Altogether, thirty thousand were killed.

The commune was crushed by wolves and swine. But it was the most glorious achievement of our time. . . . *(Walks, takes some more beer)*

Bakunin and I drank and argued, drank and argued some more. I said to him: "Mikhail, you don't understand the concept of a proletarian state. We cannot shake off the past in one orgasmic moment. We will have to remake a new society with the remnants of the old order. That takes time."

"No," he said. "The people, overthrowing the old order, must immediately live in freedom or they will lose it."

It began to get personal. I was getting impatient and I said, "You are too stupid to understand."

The brandy was having an effect on him, too. He said: "Marx, you are an arrogant son of a bitch, as always. It is you who don't understand. You think the workers will make a revolution based on your theory? They care not a shit for your theory. Their anger will rise spontaneously, and they will make a revolution without your so-called science. The instinct for revolution is in their bellies." He was aroused. "I spit on your theories."

As he said this, he spat on the floor. What a pig! This was too much. I said: "Mikhail, you can spit on my theories, but not on my floor. Clean it immediately."

"There," he said. "I always knew you were a bully."

I said, "I always knew you were a eunuch."

He roared. It sounded like a prehistoric animal. Then he leaped on top of me. You must understand, the man was enormous. We wrestled on the floor, but were too drunk to really hurt one another. After a while, we were so tired that we just lay there, catching our breath. Then Bakunin rose, like a hippopotamus rising out of a river, unbuttoned his trousers, and began to urinate out the window! I could not believe what I was seeing. "What in hell are you doing, Mikhail?"

"What do you think I'm doing? I'm pissing out your window."

"That is disgusting, Mikhail," I said.

"I'm pissing on London. I'm pissing on the whole British Empire."

"No," I said, "You're pissing on my street."

He didn't reply, just buttoned his pants, lay down on the floor, and began to snore. I lay down on the floor myself, and was soon unconscious. Jenny found us both like that, hours later, when she woke with the dawn. *(Stops to take a swallow of beer)*

No, they could not allow the commune to live. The commune was dangerous, too inspiring an example for the rest of the world, so they drowned it in blood. It still happens, does it not, that whenever, in some corner of the world, the old order is pushed aside and people begin to experiment with a new way of living—people innocent of ideology, just angry about their lives —it cannot be permitted. And so they go to work—you know who I mean by *they*—sometimes insidiously, covertly, sometimes directly, violently, to destroy it.

(Reading in the newspaper) So, they keep saying: "Capitalism has triumphed." Triumphed! Why? Because the stock market has risen to the sky and the stockholders are even wealthier than before? Triumphed? When one-fourth of American children live in poverty, when forty thousand of them die every year before their first birthday?

(Reads from the paper) A hundred thousand people lined up before dawn in New York City for two thousand jobs. What will happen to the ninety-eight thousand who are turned away? Is that why you are building more prisons? Yes, capitalism has triumphed. But over whom?

You have technological marvels, you have sent men into the stratosphere, but what of the people left on earth? Why are they so fearful? Why do they turn to drugs, to alcohol, why do they go berserk and kill? *(Holds up the newspaper)* Yes, it's in the newspapers.

Your politicians are bloated with pride. The world will now move toward the "free enterprise system," they say.

Has everyone become stupid? Don't they know the *history* of the free enterprise system? When government did nothing for the people and everything for the rich? When your government gave a hundred million acres of land free to the railroads, but looked away as Chinese immigrants and Irish immigrants worked twelve hours a day on those railroads, and died in the heat and the cold. And when workers rebelled and went on strike, the government sent armies to smash them into submission.

Why the hell did I write *Das Kapital* if not because I saw the misery of capitalism, of the "free enterprise system"? In England, little children were put to work in the textile mills because their tiny fingers could work the spindles. In America, young girls went to work in the mills of Massachusetts at the age of ten and died at the age of twenty-five. The cities were cesspools of vice and poverty. That is capitalism, then and now.

Yes, I see the luxuries advertised in your magazines and on your screens. (*Sighs*) Yes, all those screens with all those pictures. You see so much and know so little!

Doesn't anyone read history? *(He is angry.)* What kind of shit do they teach in the schools these days? *(Flashing lights, threatening. Looks up)* They are so sensitive!

I miss Jenny. She would have something to say about all this. I watched her die, sick and miserable at the end. But surely she remembered our years of pleasure, our moments of ecstasy, in Paris, even in Soho.

I miss my daughters. . . .

(Picks up newspaper again, reads) "Anniversary of Gulf War. A victory, short and sweet." Yes, I know about these short, sweet wars, which leave thousands of corpses in the fields and children dying for lack of food and medicine. *(Waves the newspaper)* In Europe, Africa, Palestine, people killing one another over boundaries. *(He is anguished.)*

Didn't you hear what I said a hundred and fifty years ago? Wipe out these ridiculous national boundaries! No more passports, no more visas, no more border guards or immigration quotas. No more flags and pledges of allegiance to some artificial entity called a nation. Workers of the world, unite! *(He clutches his hip, walks around.)* Oh, God, my backside is killing me. . . .

I confess: I did not reckon with capitalism's ingeniousness in surviving. I did not imagine that there would be drugs to keep the sick system alive. War to keep the industries going, to make people crazed with patriotism so they would forget their misery. Religious fanatics promising the masses that Jesus will return. *(Shakes his head)* I know Jesus. He's not coming back. . . .

I was wrong in 1848, thinking capitalism was on its way out. My timing was a bit off. Perhaps by two hundred years. *(Smiles)* But it will be transformed. All the present systems will be transformed. People are not fools. I remember your President Lincoln saying that you can't fool all of the people all of the time. Their common sense, their instinct for decency and justice, will bring them together.

Don't scoff! It has happened before. It can happen again, on a much larger scale. And when it does, the rulers of society, with all their wealth, with all their armies, will be helpless to prevent it. Their servants will refuse to serve, their soldiers will disobey orders.

Yes, capitalism has accomplished wonders unsurpassed in history—miracles of technology and science. But it is preparing its own death. Its voracious appetite for profit—more, more, more!—creates a world of turmoil. It turns everything—art, literature, music, beauty itself—into commodities to be bought and sold. It turns human beings into commodities. Not just the factory worker, but the physician, the scientist, the lawyer, the poet, the artists—all must sell themselves to survive.

And what will happen when all these people realize that they are all workers, that they have a common enemy? They will join with others in order to fulfill themselves. And not just in their own country, because capitalism needs a world market. Its cry is "Free trade!" because it needs to roam freely everywhere in the globe to make more profit—more, more! But in doing so, it creates, unwittingly, a world culture. People cross borders as never before in history. Ideas cross borders. Something new is bound to come of this. *(Pauses, contemplatively)*

When I was in Paris with Jenny in 1843, I was twenty-five, and I wrote that in the new industrial system people are estranged from their work because it is distasteful to them. They are estranged from nature, as machines, smoke, smells, noise invade their senses—progress, it is called. They are estranged from others because everyone is set against everyone else, scrambling for survival. And they are estranged from their own selves, living lives that are not their own, living as they do not really want to live, so that a good life is possible only in dreams, in fantasy.

But it does not have to be. There is still a possibility of choice. Only a possibility, I grant. Nothing is certain. That is now clear. I was too damned certain. Now I know—anything can happen. But people must get off their asses!

Does that sound too radical for you? Remember, to be radical is simply to grasp the root of a problem. And the root is *us*.

I have a suggestion. Pretend you have boils. Pretend that sitting on your ass gives you enormous pain, so you must stand up. You must move, must act.

Let's not speak anymore about capitalism, socialism. Let's just speak of using the incredible wealth of the earth for human beings. Give people what they need: food, medicine, clean air, pure water, trees and grass, pleasant homes to live in, some hours of work, more hours of leisure. Don't ask who deserves it. Every human being deserves it.

Well, it's time to go.

(Picks up his belongings. Starts to go, turns)
Do you resent my coming back and irritating you? Look at it this way. It is the second coming. Christ couldn't make it, so Marx came. . . .

END OF PLAY

DAUGHTER
OF VENUS

PREFACE

My first play, *Emma* (about the feminist-anarchist Emma Goldman), was what you might expect from a historian turned playwright—that is, a play based on a historical figure. After that, I began to think I should give myself a better test of the imagination and try to emulate the playwrights I most admired (Chekhov, Shaw, Ibsen, Eugene O'Neill, Arthur Miller) and write about characters that I invent. True, in most works of fiction, characters are loosely or strongly based on someone the writer has encountered or learned about. But still, the characters are fundamentally inventions of the writer and make greater demands on him or her than would be the case in writing about a historical figure.

Between the writing of *Emma* in the mid-1970s and the writing of *Daughter of Venus* in the early 1980s, I wrote my book *A People's History of the United States,* and it may be that after such an immersion (a drowning?) in history I was eager to get away from the solidity of historical fact and roam more freely through the possibilities of human character. In any case, I believe it was in such a mood that I wrote *Daughter of Venus.*

Of course, I could not possibly (given my lifelong preoccupation with issues of war, militarism, justice) stray too far from the reality of the world around me, nor could the characters in my play escape that.

I think I can identify the moment in my life when I caught a glimpse of what would be the central interpersonal conflict in *Daughter of Venus*. My wife, Roslyn, and I had encountered in Paris the daughter of a scholar we knew back home. Having moved to France, this young woman became involved in the militant activities of the French Left and was full of the energy and enthusiasm that one finds in young people of conscience who discover a cause they can believe in.

Years later, visiting the States, she came to our home and, sitting on our porch, poured out her anguish. She was disappointed in her father, who was, indeed a person of the American Left and yet who, in her view, fell short of the heroic stature she hoped for, longed for, as his daughter. There were tears in her eyes as she expressed these feelings, and while my wife and I may have thought her expectations were excessive, and perhaps no father could match them (could I?), we were moved by the depth of her feeling.

I think it was the memory of this young woman that became at least the germ of the character of Aramintha I played with when I began to write *Daughter of Venus*. I imagined an ongoing debate on stage with her father—personal, political, intellectual. Her mother, the Venus of the play—beautiful, but a statue come to life with the most human of emotions—was in some indecipherable way (and I only realized this after I began to write) modeled after my wife, Roslyn.

It was a family drama, as I envisioned it and wrote it, but the context was inescapably political, because the father in the play, the scientist Paolo Matteotti, had been, and perhaps would be again, involved in the U.S. government's deadly tests of nuclear weapons. When I wrote the play, in the 1980s, the cold war between the United States and the Soviet Union was at its height, Ronald Reagan was president, and the race for bizarre nuclear weapons, which both Democratic and Republican presidents had engaged in, was continuing.

As I contemplated reviving *Daughter of Venus* in 1990 the Soviet Union was collapsing. The political context of the play —the cold war, the arms race—had changed drastically. I lay the play aside. And then came the election of George W. Bush, the tragedy of 9/11, and a new rationale for militarism and war. The arms race would continue, except that a "war on terror" would substitute for the cold war on "Communism." The definable enemy, the Soviet Union, was now being replaced by an elusive and indefinable enemy, the terrorists. I decided that I now had a new context for the family conflict that was at the heart of *Daughter of Venus*.

DAUGHTER OF VENUS

Act One | Scene One

*Family room, living and dining room with opening to kitchen,
a door leading to study, a stair leading upstairs, a door leading to
bathroom, a hallway from outside. Lots of books, a dining table,
a piano in a far corner, which is in darkness most of the time, and
illuminated during flashbacks. There is a revolving chair, a telephone
upstage, a tape deck, art (Modigliani and Picasso prints, quite large)
on the walls, including the somewhat abstract painting of a woman.*

*Afternoon sunlight drifting in. Aramintha Matteotti sits at a
table dialing the phone. Twenty-one, twenty-two. She wears khaki
pants, blue work shirt, a jacket not really thick enough to keep her
warm, no gloves. Knapsack, suitcase nearby, suggesting she has just
come in from traveling.*

ARAMINTHA: Hello, Meadowbrook Hospital? I'd like to speak
to Mrs. Matteotti please. . . . It might be under her maiden
name, Lucy Hamilton. I think she was admitted about two
weeks ago. . . . You don't call patients to the phone? You
can't be serious. I'm her daughter *(Her voice rising)* No,
I can't wait until visiting day. I've been out of the country.
I just got—Yes, I do want to speak to her nurse. . . . Hello,
this is Aramintha Matteotti. . . . She can't be "fine" or she
wouldn't be there, right? The *head* psychiatrist? Is there any
other kind? Only joking. *(Sarcastic, angry)* Yes, I do want to

talk with him. No, I won't call back. I'll wait as long as it takes. *(Munching desperately on a cookie)* Maybe I'll write a letter to the *Times* and tell them Meadowbrook doesn't let kids talk to their parents. No, I'm not upset. Okay. Okay. *(She waits, taking a swallow of milk, another bite of a cookie.)* Mom! It's Aramintha, Mom. I'm home. Yes, it's me! I'm fine Mom. Can you hear me? Please, tell me how you are. Oh, yes, I can hear you now. You haven't been well, I know that mom. I know, yes. Did you get my letter? I sent you a letter. No, it wasn't dangerous. Not for me. It's complicated. Yes. Mom, I'll come see you on Saturday. I'll bring Jamie and Dad. Mom, I'm not fat anymore. *(She's interrupted.)* Hello, hello! *(Pushes down the receiver repeatedly. Yells)* You assholes!

> *(Aramintha starts to walk away from the phone when it rings. She answers it.)*

ARAMINTHA: Hello? No he isn't here. He's probably still in the lab at school. Who should I—Dr. John Lendl? One "e." I've got it. I'll tell him you called.

> *(She hangs up and heads back towards her milk and cookies when she hears a key in the door. It is Jamie Matteotti. He is twenty-one, dark haired, good-looking, but holds himself oddly. He is carrying a paper sack with something in it. He sees Aramintha, stops, smiles. She rushes to him, hugs him.)*

ARAMINTHA: It's so good to see you, Jamie.

JAMIE *(his speech is a little slow; he is happy)*: Aramintha! Were you on an airplane?

ARAMINTHA *(nods)*: Two airplanes. First a real tiny one—then a huge one.

JAMIE: A jet? A jumbo jet?

ARAMINTHA: Oh yes. Jamie . . . where were you just now?

JAMIE: I was working.

ARAMINTHA: Dad wrote me about your job. I used to go there for pizza.

(Jamie nods.)

ARAMINTHA: Are they nice to you?

JAMIE: Everybody likes me. Except this other busboy. He doesn't like me.

ARAMINTHA: He will too when he gets to know you.

JAMIE *(matter of factly)*: No, I don't think so. He makes fun of me. *(He giggles.)* When he's not looking I make fun of him.

ARAMINTHA: What do you do?

JAMIE *(matter of factly)*: I fart.

ARAMINTHA: You don't!

JAMIE: I do. Three times in a row. That way he knows it's me.

ARAMINTHA *(laughing, hugging him)*: Right there in the restaurant?

JAMIE: Oh no. In the kitchen.

ARAMINTHA *(shaking her head, laughing)*: Oh Jamie! *(She reaches into her knapsack, takes out a colorful cap.)* I brought you something. The people in my village made it. Just for you. I told them about you, and they said: "This is a present for your brother."

(Jamie puts it on, happily.)

ARAMINTHA: Do you want to wear it now?

JAMIE *(taking it off)*: I'll save it.

ARAMINTHA: For special occasions.

JAMIE *(he likes the phrase)*: Yeah, *for special occasions.* (He opens his paper sack, takes out flowers, gives them to Aramintha.)

ARAMINTHA: You remembered how I love flowers! They're beautiful. But you didn't expect me home until tomorrow.

JAMIE: I forgot.

(Aramintha laughs, embraces him.)

ARAMINTHA: Where did you get them?

JAMIE: Francesca says I can take anything that's left on the tables. *(He acts out cleaning off a table and whisking things into his paper sack.)* I have lots of wine bottles and corks.

ARAMINTHA: What else?

JAMIE: Eyeglasses. People take them out to read the menu. Then they leave them on the table.

ARAMINTHA: Don't they come back for them?

JAMIE: Sometimes. But when they don't come back, I keep them.

ARAMINTHA: What do you do with them?

JAMIE: I wear them sometimes. Things look different that way.
    (He takes a pair out of his pocket, puts them on.)
        (Aramintha laughs.)

ARAMINTHA: Do you still collect keys?

JAMIE: I have about a thousand keys.

ARAMINTHA: And do you still like Oreos and milk?
    (Jamie goes to the pantry and comes back, smiling, carrying a box of Oreos.)

ARAMINTHA: Good, let's save them for before we go to sleep, like we used to do.

JAMIE: Aramintha, you were gone a long time.

ARAMINTHA: Well, first I was in college. Remember I said I was going to college?
    (Jamie nods.)

ARAMINTHA: Then I went to this little village far away.
    (Jamie reaches into his pocket, pulls out a sack of postcards.)

ARAMINTHA *(laughs)*: You got my postcards!

JAMIE: Did they like you there?

ARAMINTHA: I made lots of friends, Jamie. I lived with a family. They called me their daughter.

JAMIE: You're not really their daughter.

ARAMINTHA: Not really. But they loved me and I loved them. I slept in a corner of their room. I went out in the fields and worked with them, planting things. We ate together all the time. There were parties and we would all dance.

JAMIE: If I went there would I be their son?

ARAMINTHA: Oh yes. They would introduce you to people and say: "This is our son Jamie."

JAMIE: If I was their son, would my mom still be my mom?

ARAMINTHA: Always and forever. *(She pauses.)* Jamie, I spoke to Mom on the phone. We can see her on Saturday.

JAMIE: Will she come home with us?

ARAMINTHA: I think she has to stay there until she's better.

> *(Jamie nods.)*

JAMIE: Are you going away again?

ARAMINTHA: We'll see. But I'm here for Christmas. We'll do lots of things together.

> *(Sound of door opening. Paolo Matteotti comes in, overcoat half off, carrying a briefcase.)*

PAOLO *(in a slight Italian accent)*: Aramintha! This is against the law! You're not supposed to be here until tomorrow. *(Embraces her)*

> *(Aramintha reacts a little coolly.)*

ARAMINTHA: I made a lucky connection in Mexico City.

PAOLO: You see, we can't trust the airlines. *(He examines her.)* Wait, you're not Aramintha. What happened? Nothing left to you. My God, how long did your diarrhea last?

ARAMINTHA: I'm lighter, but stronger. Every day, I walked up and down mountains for miles.

PAOLO: We'll have some good meals. I've been cooking for me and Jamie. Aramintha, I'm glad you're home. *(He shakes his head.)* It's been such a time.

ARAMINTHA: I spoke to Mom.

PAOLO *(surprised)*: You did?

ARAMINTHA: Three minutes, then they cut us off.

PAOLO: Well, they have their reasons. . . .

ARAMINTHA *(flares up)*: The bastards! Don't make excuses for them!

PAOLO *(wearily)*: Aramintha . . .

ARAMINTHA: I told her we'd come Saturday.

PAOLO: Good.

> *(Silence.)*

ARAMINTHA: Why can't she come home now?

PAOLO *(shaking his head)*: Don't you understand?

JAMIE *(blurting out)*: Mom tried to kill herself! *(Biting his nails: Aramintha is upset.)*

ARAMINTHA *(trying to control herself)*: What is it like where she is?

PAOLO: Jamie, why don't you go upstairs and watch TV?

> *(Jamie starts to go, then stops.)*

JAMIE *(showing his hat)*: Aramintha brought me that from her village.

ARAMINTHA: Jamie, try it on for Dad.

JAMIE *(shaking his head)*: It's for special occasions. *(Goes upstairs)*

PAOLO: They first put her in a state hospital. Horrible. I took her out immediately. This place, Meadowbrook, is very expensive. But decent. There's a piano near her room. They tell me she sits at it but doesn't play.

ARAMINTHA: I can't imagine her not playing the piano.

> *(The phone rings.)*

ARAMINTHA: I forgot to tell you, a man called.

PAOLO *(picks up the phone)*: Hello. John, I haven't been avoiding you. It's been very hectic. Family things . . . Yes, of course it's possible. I know—it's been a very long time. How long are you in town for? Dinner out tonight? I don't think so. My daughter is just home from overseas. Why don't you come here for dinner? Afterward we can talk alone. . . . Just a moment.

(Aramintha has slammed something down with a big bang, maybe kicked over a chair. Paolo holds the mouthpiece and with the other hand gestures as if to ask, "What's wrong?")

ARAMINTHA: I just got home! We've got to talk about Mom! Tell your friend to . . .

PAOLO: Shhh! *(Goes back to phone)* John, my daughter is just back from Guatemala. How about after dinner? Nine would be good. See you later. *(Turns to Aramintha)* John is an old associate. I haven't seen him in twenty years.

ARAMINTHA *(still fuming)*: Oh yeah. I forgot all about your associates. They come first.

PAOLO *(sternly)*: No, they don't. *(Then, more softly)* Aramintha, he's not coming until nine. You and I will have plenty of time to talk. Will you help me with dinner? *(Moves into kitchen area)* Remember, I used to cook sometimes? Wasn't that bad, was it?

ARAMINTHA *(joining him in the kitchen area)*: A little from your Italian side, a little from your Jewish side—I remember you used to make matzoh balls with spaghetti. It was always confusing to have a father who is an Italian Jew. Especially when he talks like a WASP.

PAOLO: I certainly don't talk like a WASP.

ARAMINTHA: Sometimes, on the phone, to certain people . . . *(She imitates a straight midwestern voice.)* "Hello there, George . . ."

PAOLO: You want me to talk like Chico Marx? *(He is playful, starts talking with an accent.)* Alla right, all right, you like a better? *(He stops abruptly, frowns.)* You've become so critical, Aramintha!

ARAMINTHA: I'm just speaking my mind. I never did that when I was a kid.

PAOLO: You never did?! When you were five and we were in the Guggenheim Museum, crowds of people walking quietly around, and you said in a loud voice *(imitates)*, "I'm going to throw up!" I had to hustle you out of there. You always spoke your mind, Aramintha.

ARAMINTHA: And you always hustled me out.

PAOLO *(sighs)*: Well, let's think about dinner. I prepared some eggplant for me and Jamie to have tonight. With linguine and fresh tomato sauce.

ARAMINTHA: Great! I'm dying of hunger.

PAOLO: Okay. You put the salad together. I'll boil the water for the linguine.

> *(They work in silence for a moment.)*

ARAMINTHA *(turning to him)*: Dad, *what happened?*

PAOLO: I was called out of a lecture. A doctor was on the phone. She had taken a whole bunch of sleeping pills. She was in a coma. I spent the next four days there, in the hospital, and then she came out of it. *(He is anguished.)*

> *(Aramintha puts her hands over her eyes.)*

PAOLO: The doctors said she should be hospitalized. For her own safety. I didn't want to. I wanted her home. But I was very afraid. I'm still afraid.

ARAMINTHA: But why would she . . .?

PAOLO: I don't know.

ARAMINTHA: You must know. . . .

PAOLO *(angrily)*: I said I don't know.

ARAMINTHA: How can you live with a person and not know. Didn't you see . . .?

PAOLO *(irritated)*: No, I didn't see anything.

ARAMINTHA: Maybe you were too busy. The lab, you were always . . .

PAOLO *(hostile)*: Yes, in the lab. *That's my work.* What's yours?

ARAMINTHA: Some day I'll have to work, too. But I'm not

going to drown in it. You think if a person doesn't work, it's a crime. I don't want to just work. I want to be myself.

PAOLO: You don't get paid for being yourself.

ARAMINTHA: I know. When you get paid, it's for *not* being yourself.

PAOLO: Aramintha, I don't remember you being so irritating.

ARAMINTHA: You never talked with me before. *(Pleading now)* I just want to know what happened, and you're not telling me anything. Just before she took those pills, there must have been . . .

PAOLO: There was nothing. Everything was as always.

ARAMINTHA: Maybe that's why.

PAOLO *(coldly)*: Explain that to me.

ARAMINTHA *(ignoring that, softer now)*: Did something happen between you and Mom? I always thought you were in love, really in love.

PAOLO: We were. . . . It was a romance, from the start. *(Removes his glasses)*

> *(Piano music, starting with single notes. Stage left, darkened, begins to become visible, with the figure of Lucy sitting at the piano. Paolo walks over to her. He embraces Lucy from behind. She turns around.)*

LUCY: Did you really know right away?

PAOLO: I didn't *know*, but I hoped. . . . And you?

LUCY: Before we ever spoke a word. When I saw you get up on the witness stand at the hearing. You were so young, so slight, compared to all the others. The guy from the *Post* leaned over to me . . .

PAOLO: I can understand that!

LUCY *(ignoring the remark)*: And said: "That's Paolo Matteotti, youngest of the kid geniuses on the space program."

PAOLO *(waves his hand dismissively)*: I looked out at the press gallery—a hundred reporters—you were the only one I saw. I thought, "She can't be a reporter." Your hair was down to your shoulders. You were so lovely, so healthy-looking. I wondered what you were doing there.

LUCY: I stared at you and forgot to take notes, but when I wrote my story I remembered word for word what you said. They were going back into history and some of those senators wanted to connect you with Oppenheimer to discredit your testimony. They questioned you about Oppenheimer's disapproval of the hydrogen bomb and you replied: "When the hydrogen bomb entered the world, it meant the great powers would be preparing for a holocaust which would make Hitler's acts look petty. Any decent person would have opposed it." You weren't taking any crap.

PAOLO: I knew they would pass on me anyway. They needed me to check the radiation levels.

LUCY: What you said, the intensity with which you said it— I was thrilled.

PAOLO: But what about me? Me, myself. Were you attracted? I mean physically?

LUCY: I didn't notice.

(They both laugh. They embrace passionately.)

LUCY: Are you nervous? You're shaking.

PAOLO: It's cold. How about you?

LUCY: I'm getting warm.

PAOLO: Why don't you take your clothes off?

LUCY: Why don't you?

PAOLO: I'm not good at it.

LUCY: Not good at taking your clothes off?

PAOLO: You know what I mean.

LUCY: You're a scientist.

PAOLO: That's not part of our training.

(Silence, as Lucy starts undressing.)

LUCY: Is this better?

PAOLO *(pauses)*: Yes.

LUCY: It's your turn.

PAOLO: You'll see, there's nothing under my clothes. Remember Claude Rains in *The Invisible Man*?

(Lights down on stage left. Lights up on center stage)

ARAMINTHA: How long will she have to stay?

PAOLO: Until she herself can say she wants to come home. *(Shakes his head)* And she doesn't, now.

ARAMINTHA: You've been seeing her?

PAOLO: She doesn't say anything. It's as if I'm not there.

ARAMINTHA: She sounded pretty good to me.

(Paolo shakes his head.)

ARAMINTHA: Who is this Dr. Lendl?

PAOLO: We were together on an antimissile defense. We both agreed it was a terrible idea and we wanted to prove it to the crazies around the White House. Lendl is a good man. He's a physicist. Mesons, quarks, fast particles.

ARAMINTHA: I never liked fast particles.

PAOLO *(ignoring that)*: A very good physicist. For a while he stopped doing science and spent years working for some organization—world federalism . . . peace. Then I lost track of him and heard he was back with the government. . . . Yes, he and I go way back. *(Calls out to Jamie)* Jamie! Set the table. Dinner's about ready.

(Jamie comes down and joins them. He is wearing one of his pairs of glasses.)

ARAMINTHA *(laughing)*: Jamie! How can you see through these things!

JAMIE: I can't. But it makes what you eat look very interesting.

(They start to eat.)

ARAMINTHA: Mmm! I forgot how well we ate in this family. It was only when we got invited to Mom's side of the family that we starved. Fish cakes and mashed potatoes.

PAOLO: And Wonder Bread.

JAMIE: Wonder Bread is for Wonder Boy. I'm Wonder Boy. *(Gleefully . . . he is off on one of his frequent fantasies.)* Dad, you're Wonder Man. Aramintha, you can be . . .

PAOLO: Eat your food, Jamie.

ARAMINTHA: For dessert, it was always Jello.

JAMIE: I love Jello. With all those funny things inside. *(Giggles)*

PAOLO: I never understood why your mother was so marvelously healthy, growing up on fishcakes and mashed potatoes.

JAMIE *(interrupting)*: Look, Aramintha! *(He has put on another pair of glasses.)*

PAOLO *(gently)*: Take them off. It's bad for your eyes.
        (Jamie removes them. Paolo turns back to Aramintha.)

ARAMINTHA: In Guatemala it was beans and rice. Nothing else. The children were so skinny. And look at me. I'm lucky I had so much to start with.

PAOLO: You did. When you left I thought the airline would reject you: "Sorry, over the limit."

ARAMINTHA: You were sensitive about my weight when your friends came to dinner.

PAOLO: Sensitive?

ARAMINTHA: Admit it. You would call me out of my room to introduce me, then send me off. You'd kiss me good night and say something supposedly funny, like, "She's from the Italian and Jewish side." *(Pauses, her mood changes.)* I hated that because I knew you were embarrassed by how I looked.

PAOLO: No, no.

ARAMINTHA: What about your friend, Zygmunt Zeller? I'll never forget his name. He must have weighed three hundred pounds. I always imagined him as a merger of two ordinary people, one Zygmunt and one Zeller. He couldn't fit into our armchair. I remember you got the big rocking chair for him, and after that evening it never rocked again.

JAMIE *(breaking up)*: It still doesn't rock!

ARAMINTHA: You weren't embarrassed for him. You kept inviting him to dinner as if he were deeply deprived and undernourished.

PAOLO: He was not my daughter.

ARAMINTHA: That's right. A middle-aged physicist who has been stuffing himself on mesons and protons can look like a hippopotamus. But a teenage girl can't be chubby. It doesn't allow for the proper Freudian relationship between father and daughter.

PAOLO: What in the world does Freud have to do with it?

ARAMINTHA: Your *associates* were always bringing him up in those dinner conversations. Like that psychoanalyst who used to come to the house to tell us his family troubles.

PAOLO: You mean Marvin Miller. Well, psychoanalysts need someone to talk to.

ARAMINTHA: Your friends always had matching names. Zygmunt Zeller. Marvin Miller.

(Paolo shakes his head in disbelief, a bit exasperated but unable to help being amused.)

ARAMINTHA: He would look at my school drawings and say: look how short the arms are—she's reaching out for affection. He was so full of shit!

JAMIE *(breaking up)*: Who was full of shit, Aramintha?

PAOLO: You always had a tendency to substitute scatological expressions for reasoned comment.

ARAMINTHA: Scatological! Now that's a dirty word.

PAOLO: If your education were better....

ARAMINTHA: You sent me to a fourth-rate college....

PAOLO: The third-rate colleges rejected you. . . . If your education were better you'd understand why Freud wrote about feces.

ARAMINTHA: Feces! That's very scatological.

PAOLO: Feces was one of Freud's categories.

ARAMINTHA: Well, your friends kept falling into his categories.
(Jamie has been all over Aramintha, hugging her.)

PAOLO: Jamie, don't bother Aramintha.

ARAMINTHA: He's not bothering me.

PAOLO: Jamie, you're a big boy now.

ARAMINTHA: What does that mean?

PAOLO: It means he has to learn how to behave with young women.

ARAMINTHA: I'm his sister.

JAMIE: Dad, I'm going to marry Aramintha.

PAOLO: No, Jamie, brothers can't marry sisters.

ARAMINTHA: He knows that!

PAOLO: He doesn't know. . . .

ARAMINTHA *(angry)*: Don't say that!

JAMIE: I know lots of things.

PAOLO *(softening)*: Yes, Jamie, you do know some things but . . . Let's have some ice cream. *(He starts dishing it out.)*

ARAMINTHA: God, I can't stand this!

PAOLO: Let's be clear about something, Aramintha. I've always been proud of you. When you were writing poems— I always put them up in my office.

ARAMINTHA: Except the one that got me suspended from junior high.

PAOLO: You seem to forget, I wrote a letter to the school board, defending you.

ARAMINTHA: Yeah. *(She imitates the academic voice.)* "I too am offended by her language. But she has a right to her way

of expressing herself. That is basic to our constitutional
system." You always had to apologize for being right.

PAOLO: That was exactly how I felt about the poem. The language was—I guess the only word for it is . . .

ARAMINTHA: You were embarrassed. Your generation is so
easily *embarrassed.*

PAOLO: Your generation is so *embarrassing.*

ARAMINTHA: Why aren't you embarrassed by what your associates do?

PAOLO: And what is that?

ARAMINTHA: Fast particles. Mesons. Quarks. They're quarking
all the time. Quark, quark!

JAMIE *(breaking up)*: Quark, quark!

PAOLO: Three cheers for ignorance. *(To Jamie)* All right, Jamie,
you can leave the table.

JAMIE: I'm not finished eating my ice cream.

ARAMINTHA *(blowing up)*: Why are you sending him away?
You're sending everyone away!

PAOLO *(angry)*: What do you mean by that?

ARAMINTHA: Forget it.

PAOLO: I didn't send you away, did I? You decided to go off to
Guatemala.

ARAMINTHA: Yes, I did. And I'll go back.

PAOLO: I didn't know you're going back. Why?

ARAMINTHA: I made a good friend there. He was my age, but
he was a teacher in the village.

PAOLO: This boy he . . . was your boyfriend?

ARAMINTHA: I didn't say that. But yes, I guess he was.

PAOLO: All right, no questions.

   (They eat their ice cream.)

JAMIE: Can I go upstairs and watch TV?

   (Paolo nods. Jamie goes off.)

PAOLO *(after some silence)*: So you're discovering sex. *(He reaches for the coffee.)*

ARAMINTHA: No questions, eh?

PAOLO: That's a statement. *(He pours the coffee for both of them.)*

ARAMINTHA: Not an accurate statement. I discovered sex in the twelfth grade.

PAOLO: In high school?

ARAMINTHA *(gestures with her hand, good humoredly)*: That's a question. Of course in high school.

PAOLO: Of course. *(Silence)* My God, high school! *(Sips his coffee)* Well, at least you learned *something* in high school.
    (The sounds of the TV come from Jamie's room.)

PAOLO: Jamie! Turn down the television.

ARAMINTHA *(changes the subject)*: Dad, Jamie seems better to me.

PAOLO *(firmly)*: He's exactly the same.

ARAMINTHA: He seems better than I remember.

PAOLO: The tests show no change.

ARAMINTHA *(angrily)*: Why do you have such faith in tests? I hate tests.

PAOLO: Without tests, young lady, we have no sciences.
    I don't think you believe in science. I don't understand why.

ARAMINTHA: You see, there are things science doesn't understand.

PAOLO: Your mother was the same. She distrusted facts. She was such a romantic.

ARAMINTHA *(quietly)*: Don't say *was*.

PAOLO *(shakes his head, pauses)*: Aramintha, she tried to die because . . . she is a beautiful woman, meant to live in a beautiful world. Not *this* world, this world frightened her.
    (Piano music rises. Paolo walks to stage left where the lights

are coming up on Lucy, in a different costume from the previous flashback.)

LUCY: You should be more careful on the phone, Paolo.

PAOLO: Why?

LUCY: I've heard funny sounds when we talk on the phone.

PAOLO: You think . . .?

LUCY: The FBI.

PAOLO: You're being ridiculous. We don't say anything they'd be interested in.

LUCY: Yes we do. Just yesterday you were on the phone with Jim Kolodny.

PAOLO: Well?

LUCY: You talked for half an hour.

PAOLO: Is long-windedness a crime?

LUCY: You talked about the government. Not in a friendly way . . .

PAOLO: Well, we can say what we want. This is America.

LUCY *(her voice rising)*: No, you're wrong. It's not America. It used to be America. Or maybe it never was. Or maybe it's only America until you're sixteen years old, and then you grow up and see it's like every place else.

PAOLO: But it isn't like every place else.

LUCY: In certain ways it is. Secret police. Wiretapping. Secret files kept on people. We need to be more careful.

PAOLO: I'd like to think we're dangerous Lucy, but . . .

LUCY: They don't care how dangerous we are—they just care that we exist.

PAOLO: I think you need to calm down.

LUCY: You're very calmed down, Paolo. Where is that indignation you once had?

PAOLO: I put it aside. When there's nothing you can do with your indignation, it consumes you. Lucy, the world is a mess. It won't change. You must be strong and accept that.

LUCY: I need to fight back. But I can't do it alone. *(Her hand is outstretched; Paolo doesn't move toward her.)* Help me, Paolo.

PAOLO *(coldly)*: Straighten up, Lucy, straighten up!

> *(She looks at him as if now she understands she is alone. He walks back to center stage as the lights dim on the piano area.)*

ARAMINTHA: I loved the way she played the piano. She never had to read the music. It was all inside her. I remember we would all sing together those mushy musical comedies.

> *(Piano music. Lucy, obscured, playing softly)*

PAOLO: You would sit in my lap.

ARAMINTHA *(ignoring that)*: Jamie was so happy. He liked to sit next to her on the piano bench.

PAOLO: You were such an affectionate little girl.

ARAMINTHA *(ignoring that)*: You and Mom used to dance in this room. But sometimes you couldn't find anything but rock music on the radio, so you danced to the seven o'clock news.

PAOLO: No!

ARAMINTHA: Yes! The two of you were dancing to Walter Cronkite.

PAOLO: And those cross-country trips in the summer? Jamie and you in the back of our old Chevy?

ARAMINTHA: Mom would sit sideways in the front seat and read to us. I liked that because it kept my mind off the smell of bananas.

PAOLO: Bananas?

ARAMINTHA: All across Kansas, you were eating bananas. Mom would keep peeling them for you, so you would keep driving. Gas for the car, bananas for you. The smell of bananas! Jamie and I would sit in the back and giggle, which is very hard when you're holding your nose.

PAOLO *(laughs)*: I remember all of us riding horses along the

edge of the Rockies, ten thousand feet up. You kids were
fearless on top of those horses, inches away from the edge.
Your mom, too. I was scared to death.

ARAMINTHA: You were the only one who know how high we
were—see, it's possible to know too many facts.

PAOLO: Never miss a chance do you? *(Muses)* I had forgotten
about the bananas. The summer we drove to California—
there was a pearl of a lake, eight thousand feet up into
the Sierras. Your mother didn't hesitate. She took off her
clothes, dove into that ice-cold water. She could live her
life in a mountain cabin on a lake. But every time we came
back, her wonderful laughter disappeared. She would read
the newspapers and every horror in the world became a part
of her own life.

ARAMINTHA: We would hear you arguing sometimes late at
night.

PAOLO: It wasn't always like that between us.

ARAMINTHA: I knew you loved each other. I always imagined
you and Mom as Zeus and Aphrodite.

PAOLO: Was Zeus losing his hair?

ARAMINTHA: You can look very handsome.

PAOLO: On Tuesdays and Fridays, in a certain light, maybe.

ARAMINTHA: Didn't Zeus take many forms?

PAOLO: Yes, a lion or an eagle, but not an Italian-Jewish bio-
physicist.

ARAMINTHA: But Mom didn't stop loving you. What happened?

PAOLO: Her fears. Her fears grew. We all have fears, but she
became hysterical and foolish.

ARAMINTHA *(heatedly)*: She is not foolish! She was always
reading. Tolstoy, Henry James, everybody. She's smarter
than all your scientific *associates.*

PAOLO *(firmly)*: Yes. But she began to act—inappropriately. . . .

ARAMINTHA *(with scorn)*: Oh yes, *inappropriately* . . .

PAOLO: It is a fact. People began to make fun of her. It was as if she had given up on this world. She really wanted to be on another planet. Venus perhaps. Closer to the sun. More hospitable than this earth of ours. It got worse and worse. She ended up a crazy lady.

ARAMINTHA *(shouting)*: Don't you say that about my mother!

> *(She flies at him to strike him. He holds her, restraining her, embracing her.)*

PAOLO: Aramintha! Aramintha!

> *(She breaks loose, crying, the doorbell rings. Paolo hesitates.)*

PAOLO: Come in!

> *(John Lendl enters, a big man, well-dressed, carrying an attaché case.)*

PAOLO: John, come in.

> *(They shake hands while Aramintha composes herself.)*

LENDL: This must be your daughter. *(He smiles graciously.)*

> *(Aramintha nods a greeting.)*

ARAMINTHA *(rushing out)*: I'll watch TV with Jamie. *(Exits)*

LENDL: I didn't mean to . . .

PAOLO: No, no. Sit down. A drink? Let me take your coat.

> *(He does so.)*

LENDL: If you have a bit of scotch. . . . Well, Paolo, it's been a long time.

> *(Paolo is fixing drinks, nodding.)*

LENDL: I can still see you in the plane that early morning, making your way through the crawl space. You were the only scientist we could fit into the tail.

PAOLO: And I thought I was picked for the mission because I was considered a keen observer.

LENDL: Of course that was a factor. But at historic moments like that, skinniness counts. *(Laughs)* And you wanted to go along, even though you had doubts about the whole idea of antimissile defense.

PAOLO: More than doubts, I thought it was a dangerous idea. As I recall you had doubts too.

LENDL: I did. And on that first day of tests, right after we scored a hit and could see the fireball still in the sky, everyone was shouting and laughing and congratulating one another, and you said quietly: "That was lucky. We'd better test some more." You were right. The test was a fake, set up for success. And you said: "Where can I get a jeep? I'm going over there to check the radiation levels."

PAOLO: You have a good memory.

LENDL: It was history.

(They drink, comfortable, cheerful in their reminiscence.)

PAOLO: I heard you left research and went to the World Federalists.

LENDL *(sighs)*: For three years I campaigned for one world, and disarmament. But I could see it was hopeless. I decided I would work for the same goal . . . but from the inside.

PAOLO: So you went back to work for the government.

LENDL: For the Rand Corporation, on contract to the government. Recently I became their chief security officer. And now there's something special. Your talents are badly needed.

PAOLO: You know I swore off doing anything for the government. I told them the missiles-in-space program wouldn't work, and even if they did it would only accelerate the arms race.

LENDL: But you did agree to work on radiation problems when we did the desert tests in eighty-five.

PAOLO: I felt it was a chance to save lives.

LENDL: That's exactly why we need you now. *(Pauses for effect)* There's a new weapon on the drawing boards.

PAOLO: A new weapon? There aren't enough cities in the world to be destroyed by all the bombs we have. It's madness.

LENDL: Madness or not, it's reality.

PAOLO: I'm glad I'm out of it.

LENDL: None of us are, Paolo. We're on this planet, no other. And so are our children. It's our kids we have to think of. Sure the cold war is over. But we have a new enemy— terrorism. And we can not dispense with weapons. So there is a new weapon in the works, one that can be launched from a new military base.

PAOLO (gets up, paces, shakes his head): It's madness. We already have military bases in a hundred different countries.

LENDL: Yes, but all of those bases have a common problem....

PAOLO: Those countries don't want us there.

LENDL: The governments are willing, they can be pressured. But the people in those countries—that's another matter. More and more open hostility—Korea, Japan, the Middle East. Not just hostility. Terrorism. So the problem becomes: where can we have a military base with no local opposition?

      (Paolo points to the sky.)

LENDL (enthusiastic): Precisely! Space. We have been sending vehicles into space for a long time, but we've never put weapons in space. No one has. It's an exciting idea.

PAOLO: Exciting? I would say depressing. Weapons in space? Don't you think God will be annoyed at our intrusion?

LENDL (laughs): I thought you were an atheist?

PAOLO: My mother was Jewish and my father was Catholic. I thought atheism would be a good compromise. Really, John, it's a horrifying thought.

LENDL: Yes, horrifying. There are a few of us at Rand that feel the same way, but we can't oppose it openly. There's another way. That's why we need you, Paolo. It's even worse than you think. I mentioned "new weaponry."

PAOLO: I've been reading about "bunker busters"—to destroy
deeply embedded targets. A euphemism for tactical nukes,
am I right?

LENDL: We're beyond that. There's something on the boards
which is unimaginable

PAOLO: They're insane.

LENDL: That's why we need you. They've asked for precise data
on the radiation effects. That might be sobering.

PAOLO: To incorrigible alcoholics? Do they really care about
the effects? Did they care about Hiroshima? Did they care
about Agent Orange? And all those Vietnam veterans who
got sick? And depleted uranium? When the first Gulf war
was over, they boasted: "We only suffered a few hundred
deaths." And now we know, one out of every three veterans
of that war are damaged, either physically or mentally, or
their offspring are horribly crippled.

LENDL: You're right, they don't care. But we do. We've persuaded them that any new weaponry must be accompanied
by the most precise data on biological effects, radiation
disease. It's not to their interest to have a biological catas-
trophe. This country has enough enemies, it can't tolerate
more. The whole world would turn against us. We would
have no allies, not one. They worry about that. Our job
is to make them worry. That's where your expertise is
needed. If we can come up with the data, the charting,
the graphing, making it precise and persuasive, enough
evidence to make them think it's impossible, we can make
them ditch the idea.

PAOLO: John, are you telling me you want them to give up on
that? Didn't they hire you to support them?

LENDL: Of course, but I have a mind of my own, a mind they
don't understand. They trust me because I was with them
during the cold war. I believed then in the nuclear deterrent.

But with this crazy war on terrorism, there is no deterrent.
No weapon can deter terrorists. It's a ball game they do not
understand at all. There are a few of us at Rand who have
been talking with one another, and we agree it's madness,
and we should do all we can to stop it. We call ourselves the
Heisenberg Group. Remember?

PAOLO: There's speculation he sabotaged the German atomic
project by giving them false data.

LENDL: We will be giving true data, but with the same effect.
We have a good little team. A special team.

PAOLO: And you want me on it.

LENDL: We want you to direct it.

PAOLO: Direct it? Why me?

LENDL: Because you're the best. Goddamn it, Paolo, they won't
be able to fault you. You won the Nobel for your radiation
studies.

PAOLO: I'm teaching at Columbia, you know.

LENDL: You've been buried there too long, if you don't mind
my saying so, Paolo. There's practical work to be done. For
peace. Surely you can get a leave. Rand already has the
contract. Lots of money.

PAOLO: What do you mean, "lots of money"?

LENDL: A three-million-dollar budget. Write your own
salary. Choose your own staff, your space. Generous
fringe benefits. *(Pause)* I was sorry to hear about your
wife. That must have been a blow. Her total expenses
will be covered. And you have a son too. If there are
any extra expenses there . . .

PAOLO *(quickly gets up, walks across the room, agitated, picks up
glasses)*: There are no extra expenses for Jamie.

*(Lights change. Lucy, behind a scrim, is talking to an infant
in a crib.)*

LUCY: Here, here, that's right . . . yes. . . .

PAOLO: Lucy, how long will you go on nursing him?

LUCY *(enters the main area)*: I'll know when to stop.

PAOLO: I thought, after a child is two years old . . .

LUCY: It doesn't work that way.

PAOLO: How does it work?

LUCY: There's no age, no date, so long as he's happy and I'm happy.

PAOLO: He seems overjoyed, and he may be in that mood until he's twenty.

LUCY: Well, we could set a record. I don't see why it bothers you.

PAOLO: You'd be freer.

LUCY: Look how free I am. It doesn't stop me from going anywhere. When he gets hungry I feed him, wherever I am, the subway, the movies. But I've noticed it makes you a little uncomfortable.

PAOLO: Not at all. I love to look at you when . . . Maybe I'm just jealous.

LUCY: You're not excluded.

PAOLO: But it wouldn't look right, both of us nursing on the subway. *(He sighs, tired of joking.)* I just don't understand why you are so obsessed with nursing.

LUCY: I was thinking the same thing about you. . . . *(Her tone changes, softens.)* Paolo, don't you see. . . ?

PAOLO: See what?

LUCY: Maybe it will help. Maybe it will be good for Jamie. I've been reading a lot about the effects of nursing

PAOLO *(shakes his head)*: There's no scientific basis . . . not in Jamie's situation.

LUCY *(her voice rising to a shout)*: What does science have to offer Jamie? Does it have anything to offer to make up for what it did to him?

PAOLO: I can see there's no point discussing this.

LUCY: Good. *(Exits quickly to the "baby area")* There, little one, there, sleep, sleep. . . .

> *(Paolo walks back slowly to center stage as darkness envelopes Lucy.)*

PAOLO: Even with the new weaponry, surely the radiation parameters are the same.

LENDL: No, Paolo, the old calculations are out of date. We need new guidelines. You see, this new weapon takes us into an entirely different dimension. You will not believe it until you see it. It's an astonishing leap in biophysics. You are truly needed, Paolo, not for their reasons, but for ours.

PAOLO: I would have to think about this, John. I would need more information.

LENDL: Let me start with just one thought, which is immediately, on its face, absurd. But listen. We have been using the A-bomb to trigger the H-bomb, multiplying the effect by a factor of a thousand. And so we asked: what can we use the H-bomb to trigger?

PAOLO: I don't like to hear such questions.

LENDL: We're beyond questions, into answers. Which you will help us find. *(Pulls a folder out of his briefcase)* No details here, Paolo. A summary. Enough to give you the idea. I'd like to leave it with you for a few days. . . . Let's say Monday. Perhaps by then you will want to know if you want to do this assignment. But if you need more time than that . . . *(Gestures grandly)*

PAOLO *(hesitates, then reaches for the folder)*: I'll look it over.

LENDL *(laughs)*: I knew I could count on that ferocious curiosity of yours. But keep in mind, it's to be considered top secret. Beyond top secret. In fact, it's so new it hasn't even been classified.

PAOLO: Beyond top secret? And you want to leave it? Without a security check on me?

LENDL: I told you, I'm chief security officer for Rand. I've already cleared this with the D.O.D. The files on you are up to date and clear. You had top clearance for the desert tests in eighty-five. Hell, Paolo, I know you.

PAOLO: You know I was against the fusion bomb.

LENDL *(waves his hand generously)*: So was Oppenheimer. Understandable. But when Teller went to the blackboard and did his famous demonstration of its feasibility, Oppie was admiring, and so were you. He kept walking back and forth saying: "It's so technically sweet . . ."

PAOLO: Technically sweet, yes, but . . . *(Shakes his head)*

LENDL *(quickly)*: Paolo, your humanitarianism is exactly what attracts us. In 1985 you saved lives out there on the desert. The predictions you made then are turning out to be true. . . . You said, "It will show up in twenty years."

PAOLO: I read that the government will not admit that in court.

LENDL: Well, it's a budget problem. It would lead to thousands of lawsuits by GIs.

PAOLO *(paces, thinking)*: The kind of study that I would be making—the government needs that, doesn't it, for credibility?

LENDL: Yes, but it can also be used to destroy the government's credibility.

PAOLO: And to put someone like me in charge would show good will. And be useful to the military.

LENDL: But it can also be used to block the military. Yes, I agree, it's a gamble. *(He pauses.)* There's one more fact I haven't mentioned. . . . As director of this project you will be on the president's Scientific Advisory Panel. Direct access. Henry is on that panel.

PAOLO: Henry?

LENDL: Kissinger. I may sound like name-dropping, but the truth is, after you've spent so much time with these fellows up there, you forget who they are....

PAOLO: And they forget who you are.

(Lendl laughs.)

PAOLO: What does direct access mean?

LENDL: The president has breakfast with the panel every other Tuesday.

PAOLO: A continental breakfast? It could be a short discussion.

LENDL: It usually takes at least an hour. The president likes bagels, and he has to be careful with his teeth.

(Paolo smiles.)

PAOLO *(opens the folder)*: Mind if I take a quick look now?

LENDL: Not at all . . . *(He is pleased.)*

PAOLO *(pores over the papers)*: Well does this really work out?

(He takes a pencil and a piece of paper and starts calculating.)

LENDL: Quite remarkable, isn't it?

PAOLO: Mmmm! It is ingenious. *(Makes some more calculations. Stands back, looks at what he has written, thoughtful. Turns to Lendl)* My semester does end in a few weeks.

LENDL: We've already spoken to Columbia about getting you a leave.

PAOLO: Really?

LENDL *(smiles)*: So you can see, this is not taken lightly.

PAOLO *(a slight smile on his lips)*: I can see. Another drink?

LENDL: I have a plane to catch. My driver is waiting. I'll fly back Monday to find out your decision and pick up the document. *(Smiles)* I knew you'd be fascinated, Paolo! Dinner on Monday? Eight-thirty?

(He holds out his hand. Paolo takes it. Lendl leaves.)

(Paolo turns again to the document, leafs through it, puts it in his briefcase, puts the briefcase in a drawer, uses a key to lock the case, goes to the kitchen area, opens the refrigera-

tor, takes out some milk and cookies. As he turns from the refrigerator he sees Aramintha at the little kitchen table, reading by a small lamp.)

ARAMINTHA: Hi!

PAOLO: I thought you were upstairs with Jamie.

ARAMINTHA: He's watching his favorite program. I've been reading.

PAOLO *(hesitating)*: You've been listening to our conversation?

ARAMINTHA: Some.

PAOLO: Well! *(He takes that in, looks sharply at her.)* It's an important decision. . . .

ARAMINTHA: It sucks.

PAOLO: Your usual thoughtful statement.

ARAMINTHA: It doesn't take much thought.

PAOLO: You realize this is a chance to take care in one stroke of the medical bills for your mother.

ARAMINTHA: You mean, keeping her locked up.

PAOLO: When we run out of money and credit, and she still needs help, what do we do, send her to a state institution, a chamber of horrors?

ARAMINTHA: I thought we had medical insurance.

PAOLO: Don't you know about insurance? It covers you for all things that don't happen to you. And it has a list of exceptions for all the things that do happen to you.

ARAMINTHA: So, it comes down to money, this proposition.

PAOLO: It's not that simple. If I were being asked to work on nuclear weapons, I'd refuse, of course. But if you heard right, if your brain was working—

ARAMINTHA: There you go again—bullying with your mind. . . .

PAOLO *(ignoring, angry)*:—Then you would know that there is an opportunity here to save lives, to set limits, to introduce sanity into insane discussions, to say: this is what your devices will do: so many leukemias, so many cancers of the lymph nodes, so many eyes burned out of their sockets. That needs to be known.

ARAMINTHA: They know it already and they don't care.

PAOLO: But I care. And John Lendl cares. You lump them all together. I know John. I trust him. He was with World Federalists.

ARAMINTHA: Wasn't Mussolini a socialist? Wasn't Nixon a Quaker? And Ronald Reagan probably sold Girl Scout cookies.

PAOLO: Such logic!

ARAMINTHA: Why don't you find out all that stuff on your own and publish it?

PAOLO: I don't have their resources.

ARAMINTHA: So they have you. *You* will *become* one of their resources, like you were at Los Alamos. They didn't listen to you and you felt miserable. Why did you work for them at all?

PAOLO: Someone had to declare safety levels. They were sending GIs into the test areas. I said, move them back. They were telling fairy stories to the soldiers.

ARAMINTHA: But then they used you to say, "Now it's all right. Now we know the right distances. We can go ahead." You could have told them straight out what you once told me: "*There are no right distances.*"

PAOLO *(icily)*: I had to deal with reality. We cannot all run away to Guatemala. In the real world we have to connect with people who have some power—like John Lendl.

ARAMINTHA: I met people like him in the American embassy in Guatemala City when I went to get help for our village. The army was killing people. "We're on your side," they always said. They lied to us.

PAOLO: I understand what you're saying Aramintha—but I know John.

ARAMINTHA: So you're going to do it. Why can't you turn them down and tell the world about their plans for more weapons, more weapons to kill us all? Why can't you take those plans and send them to the newspapers?

PAOLO: I'm not a hero, Aramintha.

ARAMINTHA *(crying out)*: Why not? I *want* my father to be a hero.

PAOLO: Sorry. I'm not from the outer planets. I'm from this earth, from a little village outside of Florence, Italy. Not you, you were born on Venus.

ARAMINTHA: I was born of you, too.

PAOLO: You don't feel a part of me. Your coldness saddens me.

ARAMINTHA: I have nothing to feel warm about. Mom had nothing to feel warm about.

PAOLO: She was disappointed in the world.

ARAMINTHA *(quietly)*: She was disappointed in you.

PAOLO *(angry)*: Nonsense! Absolute nonsense!

> *(He turns to stage left as piano music begins to rise and lights begin to come up on the piano area and Lucy.)*

ARAMINTHA: I've got to get some fresh air. *(She leaves.)*

PAOLO *(hears a noise, calls out)*: Jamie! Jamie! *(He walks over to where light is up on Lucy.)*

LUCY *(distraught)*: What do they say?

PAOLO *(measuring his words)*: They say medication will help him.

LUCY: What do you mean?

PAOLO: There's damage to his nervous system. That's why he has had trouble walking.

LUCY *(sobbing)*: Why don't you talk straight? You mean his *brain. (She can hardly speak.)* My God! What can be done?

PAOLO *(quietly)*: Not too much. *(Bites his lip)* He is a beautiful boy. He will have trouble learning. But he will be all right.

LUCY: It happened in Nevada, didn't it? When you agreed to
    monitor the tests.

PAOLO *(sharply)*: No, not at all. This kind of thing has been
    around for centuries. It affects a certain percentage of
    infants.

LUCY: It's from the tests. I felt it as I was carrying him.

PAOLO *(shaking his head)*: There's no way . . .

LUCY *(interrupting him)*: I *felt* it—the poison—go through
    my clothes, through my skin, into my womb, into the blood
    of my child. I *felt* it. You wanted to go there. You said it
    was safe. You were the expert. You said, "I know the right
    distances; it's safe." *(Beat)* I felt it go through me! You and
    your associates. The scientists, the experts, you all laughed
    together, drinking all night before the explosion. *And I was
    carrying your child.* All of you, liars!

PAOLO: Oh God, Lucy, please don't. . . . It will be all right.
    We will get help.

LUCY: Liars! All of you . . .

    *(Lights dim on her. Paolo walks back to center stage, as
    Jamie comes down from his room.)*

PAOLO: Aramintha said you were watching TV.

JAMIE: I wanted to ask you something.

PAOLO: Yes, what is it?

JAMIE: When I go to sleep tonight, will you lie down with me?

PAOLO: Jamie, that's what I used to do when you were little.
    Now you're a big boy.

JAMIE: No, I'm not a big boy. Not really.

PAOLO: Why do you say that?

JAMIE: Because I'm not. I don't remember things. You told me
    that I don't remember things.

PAOLO: I was wrong. You are a big boy.

JAMIE: And that's why you don't want to lie down with me
    when I go to sleep?

PAOLO: Yes, that's why.

JAMIE *(pleading)*: But I *like* you to do that.

PAOLO: We can't do everything we like.

JAMIE: You do everything you like.

PAOLO: Do I?

JAMIE: Yes, you do.

PAOLO: It's been years since I used to lie down with you when you went to sleep.

JAMIE: Mom did it before she went to the hospital. So now I have to lie down alone—except for Charles.

PAOLO *(pondering)*: Charles . . . ?

JAMIE: My kangaroo.

PAOLO: Oh, I keep confusing Charles with Robert.

JAMIE: Robert is my baboon. Don't you know the difference between a baboon and a kangaroo?

PAOLO: Yes, I do. I just don't know the difference between Robert and Charles.

JAMIE: Charles is my kangaroo.

PAOLO: I'll try to remember that. You see, Jamie, we all have trouble remembering things, not just you.

JAMIE: I am a big boy, even if I don't remember things?

PAOLO: Yes, you are.

JAMIE: But I still want you to lie down with me, even if I'm big.

PAOLO: Yes, Jamie, I will, tonight.

> *(Aramintha has returned, listens.)*

JAMIE: And tomorrow night.

PAOLO: Well, we'll talk about that tomorrow night.

JAMIE: Good, that will give us something to talk about tomorrow night! *(He goes upstairs.)*

PAOLO *(wearily)*: I'm doing my best, Aramintha. Your mother needs care. Jamie needs care.

ARAMINTHA: You mean they need to be put away. My mother is gone. Maybe Jamie will be next.

PAOLO: You're talking crazy.

ARAMINTHA: What a world! You're sane and I'm crazy.
Lendl, that creep! He's sane and Mom is crazy. The
president, who's ready to kill us all, is smart, and Jamie,
who wouldn't hurt an ant . . . *(whispers)* is *retarded*. You
and all your associates, with your facts and figures. All
those highly educated, stupid men. Fuck all of them, fuck
you too!

PAOLO *(desperately)*: Aramintha!
(He sees she is crushed and goes to her. She turns away.)

PAOLO *(weary)*: I have an early morning lecture.
*(Jamie comes down. He is wearing still another pair of
glasses.)*

PAOLO: Good night, Jamie. *(He remembers.)* Call me when
you're going to bed.

ARAMINTHA: Want some milk, Jamie? No Oreos left? *(Points
her finger accusingly to the stairs where Paolo went up)* But I
saw some graham crackers, okay?
*(He nods. They sit in silence, drinking and munching hun-
grily, fooling around, grabbing the cookies back and forth,
switching the milk, he is enjoying it enormously. The phone
rings. Aramintha picks it up, listens.)*

ARAMINTHA: Yes! Yes, we will.

PAOLO *(from upstairs)*: Who is that on the phone?

ARAMINTHA: Could you hold on a moment please? *(To Paolo)*
Meadowbrook. They've approved a trial visit. We can take
Mom home with us for the weekend.
*(Lights come up a bit on Lucy, stage left, sitting at the
piano, not playing, motionless.)*

PAOLO: Well, well! Good news, good news!

JAMIE: Aramintha, you're not fooling? Mom is coming home?

ARAMINTHA: For the weekend, they said. Just for the weekend.

(She sits at the table facing him. Quietly) Jamie, I want you to
show me all your glasses, and your bottles and your keys.

JAMIE: Here, this is one of my glasses. I have about a hundred.

*(She takes a pair of glasses from Jamie, puts them on, sits
there looking at him, and he at her with his own glasses, as
the lights go down.)*

Act Two | Scene One

Two days later, Saturday early afternoon. At rise, Aramintha and Jamie are seated on the floor playing with some of Jamie's stuff.

ARAMINTHA: Let's plan dinner. What does Mom really love?

JAMIE: Chocolate cake and ice cream.

ARAMINTHA: That's what *you* love. Okay. Let's see what the *Times* is telling us to eat this week. *(Finds the magazine section in a pile of newspapers)* Mmmm. Food, page sixty-three. *(Finds it)* Oh, here's a chicken recipe. . . . *(Reading)* "Preheat the oven to 375 degrees. Using the fingers and the hands, separate the skin from the main body of the chicken . . ." This is easy to do. *(Making a face)* "Starting at the neck, insert the fingers gradually between the neck and the body, pushing forward with the fingers, working around the breast meat and the thigh meat while loosening the skin . . ." I'm getting nauseous! We'd better think of something else.

JAMIE: Let's eat at Francesca's. Mom loves lasagna.

ARAMINTHA: *You* love lasagna. It's still a good idea. But we'll bring it home. Then we can have our own dessert.

JAMIE: Chocolate cake and ice cream.

> *(The phone rings. Paolo comes into the room and picks it up.)*

PAOLO: Hello. Yes, John. You're still coming Monday. . . .
   Today? No, we're driving up to Meadowbrook this after-
   noon. My wife is coming home for the weekend. *(Listens)*
   It's in my study. . . . You're not serious. *(His manner changes.)*
   That's hard to believe. . . . No, absolutely not. Let me check.
   Just a moment. Hang on. *(Looks in his desk drawer)* It's right
   there, John, in my briefcase. . . . I know, the coincidence is
   too great. I'm baffled. Well, come as soon as you can, then.
   We have to leave at four. *(Hangs up, thoughtful, upset, turns
   to the kids. His manner changes: abrupt, interrogating.)* Was
   anyone in the house besides you yesterday after I left?
       *(They shake their heads. Silence. He looks at them search-
       ingly.)*
PAOLO: Jamie, did you go into my study?
       (Jamie is silent.)
PAOLO *(sharp, threatening)*: Jamie!
       (Jamie giggles.)
PAOLO: Did you go into my desk?
JAMIE: We found the key. I showed Aramintha all my keys and
   we found it.
PAOLO: You went into my desk.
ARAMINTHA: We did.
JAMIE: We both did. I have keys to everything. *(Giggling)*
PAOLO *(excited, all that follows is fast and loud)*: It's no joke!
       (He grabs Jamie's arm hard, hurtfully.) It's no joke!
JAMIE *(crying)*: You're hurting me!
ARAMINTHA *(shouting)*: Leave him alone!
PAOLO *(angrily)*: Jamie, didn't I tell you to never, never to open
   my desk with your keys?
JAMIE: I forgot.
PAOLO *(uncontrolled anger)*: How many times did I tell you
   that?
ARAMINTHA: Stop it! I asked him to do it.

PAOLO *(turning to her, furious)*: Why? What's wrong with you? Are you crazy? Did you open my briefcase? Did Jamie have a key to that?

ARAMINTHA: I took the briefcase to Mr. Ferrari at the hardware store. I told him you lost the key. He picked the lock. . . . He said he'll send you the bill.

PAOLO: Send me the bill! *(Trying to contain his anger)* Jamie, you can go upstairs and watch your Saturday programs.

JAMIE *(still sniffling)*: I won't go until you say you're sorry. You hurt me.

PAOLO: I'm sorry, Jamie. Now you go upstairs.

JAMIE: I don't want to go.

ARAMINTHA *(putting her arms around Jamie)*: You don't have to go if you don't want to.

JAMIE: I want to go. *(He leaves.)*

PAOLO *(turns to Aramintha, furious)*: What did you do with those papers before you put them back?

ARAMINTHA: I copied them. There's a machine in the public library.

PAOLO *(shouting)*: You photocopied them! A top-secret document! What's wrong with you? Are you out of your mind! How many copies did you make?

ARAMINTHA: Only one. I ran out of dimes.

PAOLO: Ran out of dimes! What did you do with the copy?

ARAMINTHA: I took the subway down to the *Times* building. I found the office of the executive editor and gave it to the secretary. I said: "It's authentic," and I left. I hope the editor got it.

PAOLO: He did. Aramintha, *do you know what you've done?*

ARAMINTHA: I've stopped you from working for them.

PAOLO: Yes, I'm sure you have. You've also broken the law.

ARAMINTHA: I said: "Tough shit."

PAOLO: You can go to prison.

ARAMINTHA: For saying "tough shit"?

PAOLO: For giving out secret documents.

ARAMINTHA: They won't put me in jail. I'm just a kid.

PAOLO: They put the Rosenbergs in the electric chair, parents of two small children.

ARAMINTHA: They can't do it to me. I don't believe in capital punishment.

PAOLO: You're very witty. Don't you know the White House and all those people down there are hysterical about secrecy? And they are ruthless.

ARAMINTHA: They're the people you want to work for.

PAOLO: Why are you doing this?

ARAMINTHA *(crying)*: Because I don't want my mother to die.

PAOLO: Don't you think your feelings are mine too? *(Anguished)* But feelings are not enough. We will need all of our intelligence, all our strength. The world out there is without pity. Our problem is to outwit them, to survive.

ARAMINTHA: But you don't just want to survive. You want to win the Nobel Prize or something. You miss those good times in Los Alamos. I heard your friend Lendl. New weapons system! Everyone should know what they're up to. That's why I took those papers.

PAOLO *(softly)*: You don't know your facts, Aramintha.

ARAMINTHA: I know a *few* things. I don't like to overload my brain. It stops me from thinking.

PAOLO: Did you ever hear of Savonarola?

ARAMINTHA: Is this another test?

PAOLO: Savonarola lived in Florence.

ARAMINTHA: Oh, you knew him.

PAOLO: In the fifteenth century.

ARAMINTHA: You just missed him.

PAOLO: He was a monk and a prophet. He followed his feelings. But he had no power. They burned him at the stake

and spread his ashes in the river Arno. Have you read
Machiavelli?

ARAMINTHA: Of course. I'm a college-educated person.

PAOLO: Machiavelli said: "An unarmed prophet is doomed."
You must get close to power.

ARAMINTHA: In my philosophy class we read Machiavelli,
and also Thomas More. Have you read Thomas More?

PAOLO *(wearily)*: Revenge, eh? Yes, I have read More's *Utopia*.
(Pauses) Not recently.

ARAMINTHA: You never admit to not having read something.
It's always "not recently."

PAOLO: You were born recently, so naturally you've read everything recently. *(Impatiently)* What about Thomas More?

ARAMINTHA: He said: when you join the king's council, it's
a way of silencing you—you won't be able to disagree with
his policies. You'll be powerless.

PAOLO: I don't remember that.

ARAMINTHA: Well, that's what he said. Take my word for it.
I got an A.

PAOLO: You may have gotten an A, but Thomas More got an F.
He was beheaded.

ARAMINTHA: They were tough graders in those days. Well,
Machiavelli died of poisoning.

PAOLO: I never heard of that. Poisoning? From what?

ARAMINTHA: Licking asses.

PAOLO: How did you develop such respect for intellectuals?

ARAMINTHA: By being around them. Aren't intellectuals *used,*
like Machiavelli? They used all those smart guys, Oppenheimer and the others, you, to build the bomb. And then
they used you for those tests in the desert.

PAOLO *(angry)*: Don't you remember what I was doing in those
tests?

ARAMINTHA: Not really.

PAOLO: You should work on your memory. I was there to protect people.

ARAMINTHA: No, you were there so they could say, "See, it's okay, Paolo Matteotti says it's okay. So now we can take the proper precautions, and build more bombs."

PAOLO: What would you have me do? Refuse to check the radiation levels? Wouldn't that be utterly stupid? What good would that do?

ARAMINTHA: It might cause other people to refuse to work on these things, the things that *cause* the radiation levels.

PAOLO: You're dreaming, Aramintha.

ARAMINTHA: Didn't your hero Einstein say: "Governments will only stop making war when we all refuse to cooperate with them?" He *did* say something like that.

PAOLO: I don't remember that.

ARAMINTHA: You should work on your memory.

PAOLO: Don't you understand, Aramintha, this is a chance to get close to those making the decisions. All those friends of yours, yes, and friends of mine, shouting in the night. No one hears them. Your mother cried out again and again. No one listened. It drove her insane.

ARAMINTHA *(her voice rising)*: She's not insane.

PAOLO *(his voice rising too)*: Face facts. *(Being scientifically precise)* She is now, at this moment . . .

ARAMINTHA *(shouting)*: Don't you call her that, you . . .

PAOLO *(waits for her to subside)*: All right, all right . . . Don't you see, Aramintha, we can't cut ourselves loose from where power is. We're not strong enough by ourselves.

ARAMINTHA: There are millions of us, and only a few of them.

PAOLO: It's not numbers. It's power, Aramintha. Good cannot prevail over power. With all my good will, I've had no effect.

ARAMINTHA: You could have spoken out.

PAOLO: Small potatoes, Aramintha.

ARAMINTHA: You told me once that in nature, little things so small you can't see build up and build up and suddenly a miracle takes place, but it's not really a miracle, just an accumulation of lots of little things.

PAOLO: That does sound like a vulgarization of something I said.

ARAMINTHA: A vulgarization! I'm so ashamed!

PAOLO: It's a sentiment, not an analysis.

ARAMINTHA: Must everything be analyzed?

PAOLO: Yes, of course. Yes.

> *(He stops and reflects, as piano music is heard and lights come up on stage left. He walks to Lucy, playing the piano on stage left.)*

LUCY: What a wonderful movie!

PAOLO: You really liked it?

LUCY: Didn't you?

PAOLO: It was all right. A little slushy.

LUCY: What does that mean?

PAOLO: Softheaded, silly, sentimental.

LUCY: I guess I'm just softheaded, silly, sentimental.

PAOLO: It could have been a little closer to reality.

LUCY: Reality is so hateful.

PAOLO: It's all we've got.

LUCY: No, it isn't. We've got imagination, fantasy, mystery— isn't that what art is about?

PAOLO: And you consider that film art?

LUCY: Yes. The children loved it.

PAOLO: Good. I'm glad you all enjoyed it.

LUCY: You don't sound glad.

PAOLO: There was a logical flaw in the plot. Do you remember in the beginning, when . . .

LUCY: Stop it, Paolo! Really, you're spoiling everything. I don't want the children to hear this.

PAOLO: They should learn to think rationally, critically. The film was really quite ridiculously impossible.

LUCY *(shouting)*: No, no, it's all possible.

PAOLO: But . . .

LUCY: Stop it, stop talking!

PAOLO: My God, Lucy, what's wrong, what's wrong?

(Lights dim, Paolo walks back center stage.)

ARAMINTHA: You and Mom always said: think for yourself.

PAOLO: Surely you weren't *thinking* when you took that document. You have cost me a chance to do something I want very much to do.

ARAMINTHA: Why should I care?

PAOLO: You care about decisions made in Washington, decisions about war and peace. I can have access to those channels.

ARAMINTHA: Channels? It's a maze you get lost in.

PAOLO: I don't get lost easily, Aramintha. There's also the practical aspect. I know you don't concern yourself with these things, but my salary now goes to pay the hospital bills for Lucy.

ARAMINTHA: The discussion always seems to come back to money.

PAOLO *(angrily)*: Yes, money! Your education is a matter of money, your bicycle, your clothes, your milk and cookies. Why did you involve Jamie?

ARAMINTHA: He wanted to.

PAOLO: He had no idea what he was doing.

ARAMINTHA: He knows more than you think. You don't give him any credit at all. Not at all. You can't stand that he'll never be a brilliant scientist, can you?

PAOLO: Stop that.

ARAMINTHA: It's true isn't it?

PAOLO: We must face the facts about Jamie.

ARAMINTHA: He's a living being, and you can't hold him down with *facts*.

PAOLO: He's not able to deal with matters like this.

ARAMINTHA: Bullshit!

PAOLO *(sighing)*: Ah, your command of the language! Why did you do it, Aramintha?

ARAMINTHA: I didn't want mother to come home and find you working in military things again.

PAOLO: You'd rather have her come home and find her daughter indicted under the Espionage Act and her husband looking like a fool.

ARAMINTHA: That might make her better.

PAOLO: It will take more than that.

ARAMINTHA: You once told me, it's a very small distance from sanity to insanity.

PAOLO: Yes, but not back to sanity.

ARAMINTHA: But they're the ones who are really insane, aren't they, making all those bombs?

PAOLO: Perhaps not insane, but misguided.

ARAMINTHA: Oh, that makes me feel better. When the missiles start flying, they won't be insane, just misguided.

PAOLO: Not all those people at the top are evil. Even the president, he's a human being after all.

ARAMINTHA: Maybe he was, before he became president. But I see him on TV, smiling, and I think: he doesn't care if I live or die.

PAOLO: You seem to think the government is naturally evil.

ARAMINTHA: I think all governments are naturally evil.

PAOLO: I happen to know some people in Washington who do care.

ARAMINTHA: The ones who care, they don't stay, do they? Like your friend George Kisty?

PAOLO: Once he left the president's advisory council, what could he accomplish then?

ARAMINTHA: Mom said he inspired people all over the country.

PAOLO: How many? A hundred, a thousand?

ARAMINTHA: You once said to me . . .

PAOLO *(exasperated)*: My God! Will you never forget the things I said to you?

ARAMINTHA: You said: "Small numbers can have remarkable power." You talked geometric progression—how you start with just two and soon it's sixteen and then it's a hundred thousand. You said this was behind atomic power. You said it was the secret of life. . . .

PAOLO: I'm impressed with what you remember, Aramintha.

ARAMINTHA: But you've *decided.*

PAOLO: I might be able to do a little good, raise a few disturbing questions.

ARAMINTHA: You know they don't want to be disturbed. You'll disappear inside the belly of the monster, like all your friends—swallowed up, digested, and then, eliminated. You'll be . . . *feces.*

PAOLO: It's worth a try.

ARAMINTHA: So, you think you'll get the job anyway. You'll say, sorry, it's my nutty daughter. Then you can go to meetings in Washington and sit around having drinks with your pals, like in the good old days of the Project.

(The doorbell rings.)

ARAMINTHA: That must be your friend, Lendl.

(Paolo goes to her, she turns away.)

ARAMINTHA: Tell Lendl he wins out over this nineteen-year-old kid. *(She is almost in tears. Then, desperately)* Get him out of here soon. We have to go get Mom at four o'clock. *(She is anguished.)*

> *(Paolo tries to put his arm on her. She violently pulls away.)*

ARAMINTHA *(calls upstairs)*: Jamie! Let's go for a walk!

> *(Jamie races down.)*

ARAMINTHA *(calling out as they leave)*: We'll be back in time.

LENDL *(enters)*: Hello, Paolo *(Shaking hands)* Was that your daughter? And your son?

PAOLO: Yes. Make yourself comfortable.

> *(Lendl takes off his coat, folds it carefully on a chair, sits down.)*

PAOLO: I wanted her to stay so she could explain what happened.

LENDL: So, it was on this end. I'm relieved—better an unpleasant explanation than a mystery. Well, Paolo . . .

PAOLO: It's a bit bizarre. How about a drink? *(He brings out the whiskey and glasses, puts them near Lendl.)* You must understand, my daughter is very upset right now. My son collects keys. It's his hobby. They got into my room. Then she took the briefcase to a neighborhood locksmith, who opened it. Then she photocopied the paper in the public library, put the original back. If you hadn't phoned me I'd never have suspected anything.

LENDL *(sips his drink)*: How many copies did she make?

PAOLO: One. She ran out of money.

LENDL *(laughing)*: So, the capitalist system does have its good points. What if everything were free? We'd have no controls.

PAOLO: If everything were free, why would we need controls?

LENDL: So people wouldn't take advantage of their freedom.

PAOLO: Then they wouldn't really be free. . . .

LENDL *(laughing, pouring another drink)*: Paolo, this reminds

me of the old days. You and I would always have these
marvelous duels.

PAOLO: What will the *Times* do with the document?

LENDL: Nothing.

PAOLO: You're sure?

LENDL: They contacted us as soon as they got it. Aside from
the Pentagon Papers business, they've always been cooperative in matters of national security, going back to the Bay
of Pigs. You know why we can't afford to have it public.

PAOLO: Yes, the public might get frightened. I was myself, John,
as I read it.

LENDL: Of course. We all should be frightened. But I like to
think our little team can make a difference. We want to save
people from the effects of radiation. You know what those
effects are, Paolo. We're talking about that bleeding through
all the body openings that comes with radiation sickness.

PAOLO: But if there's no weapon, there's no radiation. If we
find the weapon can be made with minimum radiation
they will go ahead. We will be making the weapon possible
by our work.

LENDL: They will make the weapon with us, or without us.
We can try to eliminate its worst effects.

PAOLO: Einstein, after World War One, he was horrified when
he saw nations gathering in Geneva to outlaw certain
weapons. He said: war cannot be humanized, it can only
be abolished. The history of warfare has proved him right.

LENDL: History is not a guide any more, Paolo. On August six,
1945, we left history behind. Yes, Einstein was right. War
cannot be humanized. But our little team can stop this new
weapon in its tracks.

PAOLO: My daughter thought she could do it in her own way.

LENDL: I suppose I should not have been surprised. We're not
unaware of your daughter's history. . . .

PAOLO: I suppose that means you're *aware* of it . . . *(Laughs)*
. . . not *unaware*! I still get a kick out of the English
language. You checked with her school.

LENDL: Yes, but . . . it's not the fifties. The witch hunts are over.
We know about your wife's activism in the antinuclear
movement. My wife might have done the same.

PAOLO: What about *my* activity?

LENDL *(surprised)*: There's nothing in the record. . . .

PAOLO *(smiling)*: Your security slipped up. I once walked on a
picket line. Lucy persuaded me to come with her. I walked
along, feeling foolish. I prayed I wouldn't be asked to carry
a sign. Sure enough, this young woman stuck a sign in my
hands and walked away before I could protest. I carried it
about half an hour before I had the nerve to turn it around
and read what it said. It said: "Lesbian from Hoboken
against Nuclear Weapons."

(Lendl laughs heartily.)

PAOLO: I quickly handed it to someone else, a nice gray-haired
lady. I said: "I'm not from Hoboken." Lucy got a kick out of
that.

(Lights change as Lucy enters.)

LUCY: You got a call just before you came home.

PAOLO: Why didn't you tell me?

LUCY: I just did.

PAOLO: Who was it?

LUCY: That same man who called last week. He wouldn't give
his name. Said he'd call later. I didn't like that.

PAOLO: Call later? Tonight?

LUCY: I think so.

PAOLO: You think so. Didn't he say?

LUCY: I'm not your secretary.

PAOLO: No, of course not.

LUCY: I didn't like him. What does he want?

PAOLO: I don't know. I haven't had a chance to talk with him. Let's forget it. *(Picks up his book)*

LUCY: Do you know how many evenings we have spent this way?

PAOLO: Quarreling?

LUCY: I don't mean that. *Reading.* You reading, me reading.

PAOLO: It must be a large number. Is that bad?

LUCY: What do you think?

PAOLO: By the way you ask that question, I know what you think. I'm surprised. You love to read.

LUCY: Yes, I love to read. But sometimes . . . You and I haven't *danced* in a long time.

PAOLO: You can't imagine Fred Astaire and Ginger Rogers spending a quiet evening at home, reading?

LUCY: *They* deserve a rest. But you and I . . .

PAOLO: I seem to remember dancing very recently.

LUCY: Not with me.

PAOLO: I often confuse you with my other dancing partners— Eleanor Powell, Rita Hayworth. . . . Let's dance now.

LUCY: I don't want you to dance to please me. I want it to be spontaneous. I want you to feel like dancing.

PAOLO: I'm beginning to feel it . . . an irresistible, spontaneous urge.

> *(He begins to hum, gets up, goes to Lucy, pulls her up,*
> *she goes to him, they dance to "Let's Face the Music and*
> *Dance" until the tune ends. Lucy goes back to her book.)*

LUCY *(smiling)*: That was fun!

PAOLO: So why are you going back to your book?

LUCY: That was just right. Thank you, Paolo.

PAOLO: So *you're* satisfied. "Thank you, Paolo." You lead me on and then . . . *(He goes to her, puts his arms around her.)*

LUCY: Go back to your reading, Paolo. I am really into this book.

(He kisses her neck, shoulders, while she continues to read.)

LUCY: Let me finish this chapter.

(He doesn't stop. She drops the book and turns to him. The phone rings.)

LUCY: Don't answer it.

PAOLO: It's probably . . .

LUCY: Don't answer it.

(They are in an embrace. The phone keeps ringing.)

PAOLO: It's *annoying.*

LUCY: Ignore it.

PAOLO: Just a second.

(As he approaches telephone, it stops ringing. He comes back to Lucy. She is reading, her back turned. He watches her, while the lights go down and he turns slowly towards center stage.)

PAOLO: Have another drink.

LENDL: I've had too many. Well, one more. *(Drinks, muses)* I spent three years, Paolo, working for world peace. Then I realized that these people in the White House, in the Pentagon, really don't care about world peace. They keep saying: "It's time to kick ass."

PAOLO: The Joint Chiefs of Staff always did have a poetic streak.

LENDL *(smiling)*: Paolo, we'll have some good times together. I can see that. Like in the old days. *(Puts down his drink)* But please, try to remember, while some of our pacifist friends are making admirable moral arguments, the guys up there at the top are playing hardball.

PAOLO *(holding up a finger like a teacher)*: And kicking ass.

(Lendl doesn't know whether or not to smile. There is a noise at the door.)

PAOLO *(pauses)*: I did ask Columbia for the leave.

LENDL: Good! Good! Well, I know you're pressed for time.

PAOLO: We're supposed to start out for Meadowbrook at four.

> *(Aramintha and Jamie come in. Jamie scoots upstairs.)*

LENDL: Hello, Aramintha, your father and I have had a good talk.

ARAMINTHA: I'm sure.

PAOLO: Let's take another moment. Sit down, John. You, too, Aramintha. I just want you to know John Lendl a little.

LENDL: Just to see if I'm really a monster. *(Smiles charmingly)* My own children need to be convinced, too. Believe me, Aramintha, there are times when I think we are all monsters.

> *(She starts to sit down on his coat.)*

LENDL: I think my coat is in your way.

ARAMINTHA: No problem. *(She starts to move his coat and, feeling something, pulls out a gun.)*

LENDL: I'll take that.

ARAMINTHA: Hey look! A gun!

LENDL: It's not a toy. You'd better give it to me. *(Holds out his hand)*

> *(Aramintha moves away.)*

PAOLO: Put it back, Aramintha.

ARAMINTHA: It's real! Wow! *(She holds it, dances around with it.)* You carry a gun!

LENDL: This is New York. I've always got some classified material with me. Please put it down.

PAOLO: Put it back in Dr. Lendl's pocket, Aramintha.

ARAMINTHA: I just want to hold it a minute. I never held a real gun before. You don't mind, do you, Dr. Lendl?

LENDL: I think I do. It's not very nice of you, Aramintha, to take my gun out of my coat.

ARAMINTHA: It's not very nice of you to bring a gun into our
house.

PAOLO: Now put it back! *(He moves towards Aramintha.)*

LENDL: Don't, Paolo, it's loaded. We don't want a scuffle. She'll
give it back.

ARAMINTHA: I'm not pointing it at anyone. What's that word?
I'm deploying it, just deploying it. *(She is going to move
around and play with it, never pointing it.)*

PAOLO: Okay, enough.

ARAMINTHA: Let's say I'm protecting you. This is a bad neighborhood. Isn't that what you guys say? "We're protecting
you. You've got nothing to worry about."

LENDL *(sighing)*: I'll let you handle it, Paolo.

ARAMINTHA: Why are you so nervous? Now you know how we
all feel about those bombs.

LENDL: Okay, we can talk this out. It's not the same situation,
Aramintha. You've never handled a gun. Our weapons are
in the hands of experts.

ARAMINTHA: I hear your experts lost four hydrogen bombs
over Spain. That seems careless.

PAOLO: If you want to talk, Aramintha, fine. But first put that
down.

ARAMINTHA: No, this way I can talk from a position of
strength.

LENDL: It's not quite equal. You have a gun and we don't.

ARAMINTHA: Yes, but you weigh twice as much as me. Without
it you would overwhelm me with your conventional arms.
I need a deterrent, don't I? How much *do* you weigh?

PAOLO: I'm getting angry, Aramintha.

LENDL: It's okay, Paolo. We can discuss things calmly. She's an
intelligent girl.

ARAMINTHA: Let's say I'm as intelligent as the Joint Chiefs of

Staff. Does that give you confidence? You see, if you have a dangerous weapon, it may be turned on you.

LENDL: If you're trying to represent reality, I would have a gun too.

ARAMINTHA: Then one of us would say, "Your gun is a six-shooter and mine is a five-shooter. I want a ten-shooter." Even though you can kill with one bullet. Isn't that how it is?

LENDL: You're simplifying a very complex situation.

ARAMINTHA *(getting worked up)*: Who's simplifying? The terrorists versus the good guys. East versus West. The clash of civilizations. Us or them. Die for liberty. You call that complex thinking? I just came back from Guatemala, where tiny kids die every day because there's no medicine, and we've been spending trillions of dollars . . .

LENDL: Not trillions, Aramintha. The exact number . . .

ARAMINTHA: Okay, I'm not good at exact numbers.

PAOLO: Aramintha, we'll have to be leaving soon.

ARAMINTHA: I know how much time we have.

LENDL: Aramintha, you aren't well enough informed to make judgments on these things.

ARAMINTHA *(interrupting)*: I don't know anything. You guys know it all. You have all the details, all the figures, you have the charts, the graphs, you're so *well informed*, and you've screwed everything up all over the world.

LENDL: You have the luxury to say what you want, without consequences. Our leaders making decisions in Washington are responsible for two hundred million people. *They represent a nation.* Who do *you* represent?

ARAMINTHA *(slowly, quietly, after a pause)*: I represent my mother.

LENDL *(is silent a few seconds, then, shakes his head)*: Aramintha,

I can see you're very upset. You should try to get some
counseling.

ARAMINTHA: So, I'm crazy. For holding a gun for five minutes
with three people in the room. You guys are not crazy, but
you've been holding a gun to the heads of the whole world
for years. You're so mature, so *responsible*. But it's always the
kids who die, isn't it?

LENDL *(for the first time, taking a fanatical tone)*: I have children
of my own, Aramintha. My daughter is almost your age and
I love her dearly. I'm working for her.

ARAMINTHA: Does she think so? Who are you to decide for
her? And for me, and for everybody? Are you and the
president and all those faces on TV to decide who should
die for what? Maybe your daughter wants to decide for
herself. Maybe I do. We're not afraid. We'll figure out a
way to defend ourselves against the terrorists, against you
too. We're not afraid. You're all a bunch of cowards, with
all your bombs. *(She is crying.)*

LENDL *(stands: he's had enough)*: I'll give you three seconds
before I take it away from you.

PAOLO *(quietly, firmly, his voice is different)*: Stay away from her,
John.

ARAMINTHA: Why does everyone always count to three? Why
not seven?

LENDL: One . . .

PAOLO *(sharply)*: John!

ARAMINTHA: Excuse me, I have to go to the bathroom. *(Races
into the bathroom and shuts the door)*

PAOLO *(goes after her, bangs on the door)*: Aramintha! Come out,
don't do anything stupid.

   (Aramintha emerges, holding out empty hands.)

PAOLO: Where's the gun?

ARAMINTHA: I flushed it.

LENDL: This is really absurd!

PAOLO: Aramintha!

ARAMINTHA *(breezily)*: It didn't go down. Dad, we've got to get our toilet fixed. *(She shrugs.)* I guess I've never been good at flushing guns. *(To Lendl)* Okay, you can do what you want to me now. I've unilaterally disarmed.

> *(Paolo goes after the gun, brings it back, hands it to Lendl. Lendl takes it gingerly.)*

PAOLO *(cheerily)*: It's okay. The water is clean this time. Usually, when we have a toilet blockage . . .

LENDL *(putting on his coat)*: Paolo, let's talk when your family life is calmer. It's been an astounding day. The offer is still there. Let's talk next week.

> *(Paolo is silent.)*

LENDL *(looking directly at him)*: I mean that. Let's forget about what happened today. I have truly been looking forward to working with you again.

PAOLO: You know that proverb: if someone says, let's go fishing, make sure you're not the worm.

LENDL: This is a chance, Paolo, to be one of the fishermen. You could do big things, Paolo. What can you do outside? I'm talking about real access. I'm . . .

PAOLO: John, have you read Thomas More?

LENDL *(puzzled)*: More's *Utopia?* Not recently.

> *(Paolo and Aramintha look at one another, smiling.)*

LENDL *(shaking his head, bewildered, starts to leave, turns)*: Frankly, Paolo, your whole family is a little strange. We'll talk next week.

> *(Paolo shakes his head. Lendl leaves.)*

PAOLO: I think I need a stiff drink.

ARAMINTHA: How about some milk and Oreos?

PAOLO *(in an exaggerated Italian accent)*: That's-a just what I was thinking about. *(He calls out.)* Jamie! It's almost time to go. Come on down.

ARAMINTHA: We still have half an hour.

(Jamie comes down, fully clothed, with winter coat, scarf.)

PAOLO: Jamie, you don't have to get dressed yet.

(The light is beginning to come up, stage left, on Lucy.)

JAMIE: I want to be ready. If we're late, maybe they'll say: "She can't go home today."

PAOLO: We won't be late. We have time for a little snack to hold us until dinner.

(Jamie sits down, removes from his pocket the hat Aramintha brought for him, puts it on. Paolo watches him silently.)

ARAMINTHA: It's just for the weekend.

JAMIE *(takes glasses from his packet, puts them on)*: Maybe, if she likes the lasagna.

(Aramintha hugs him.)

PAOLO *(after a short pause)*: Maybe we should get there a little early.

(Aramintha takes a position behind and between Paolo and Jamie and envelops them both in a unifying embrace.)

END OF PLAY